**Second Edition**

# RATIONAL EMOTIVE
# BEHAVIOUR THERAPY
## in a nutshell

**GOVERNORS STATE UNIVERSITY
UNIVERSITY PARK, IL**

**SAGE** has been part of the global academic community since 1965, supporting high quality research and learning that transforms society and our understanding of individuals groups, and cultures. SAGE is the independent, innovative, natural home for authors, editors and societies who share our commitment and passion for the social sciences.

Find out more at: **www.sagepublications.com**

Michael Neenan and Windy Dryden

Second Edition

# RATIONAL EMOTIVE
# BEHAVIOUR THERAPY
in a nutshell

Los Angeles | London | New Delhi
Singapore | Washington DC

COUNSELLING IN A NUTSHELL SERIES Edited By Windy Dryden

© Michael Neenan and Windy Dryden 2006, 2011
First edition published 2006
This second edition published 2011

SAGE Publications Ltd
1 Oliver's Yard
55 City Road
London EC1Y 1SP

SAGE Publications Inc.
2455 Teller Road
Thousand Oaks, California 91320

SAGE Publications India Pvt Ltd
B 1/I 1 Mohan Cooperative Industrial Area
Mathura Road
New Delhi 110 044

SAGE Publications Asia-Pacific Pte Ltd
33 Pekin Street #02-01
Far East Square
Singapore 048763


**Library of Congress Control Number available**

**British Library Cataloguing in Publication data**

A catalogue record for this book is available from
the British Library


ISBN 978-0-85702-331-5
ISBN 978-0-85702-332-2 (pbk)


Typeset by C&M Digitals (P) Ltd, Chennai, India
Printed in India at Replika Press Pvt Ltd
Printed on paper from sustainable resources

# Contents

Preface   vi
Acknowledgement   vii

1   The distinctive features of rational emotive behaviour therapy   1

2   The REBT 'Situational ABC' model   18

3   Assessment   37

4   Disputing   47

5   Homework   60

6   Working through and promoting self-change   74

Appendix 1   Thinking distortions and their realistic alternatives   99
References   106
Index   110

# Preface

Our aim in the second edition of the book remains the same as in the first edition: to cover all of the key elements of REBT theory and practice in as few words as possible. We are often asked to compare REBT with CBT, a question we find problematic. We explain our difficulty with this question in the newly written Chapter 1 and instead we have outlined REBT's distinctive theoretical and distinctive features in that chapter.

In the practice chapters (3–6), we have preserved the 'succinct and no-frills introduction to REBT' approach. However, we have somewhat departed from this approach in the newly written Chapter 2. Since understanding REBT's 'ABC' model is so central to understanding this approach, we have chosen to use more professional jargon in this chapter to help you understand important distinctions, e.g. between rational and irrational beliefs.

Otherwise, we continue to hope that this book acts as a counterweight to and relief from the lengthy and sometimes complicated texts that trainees are required to read as part of a standard training course in REBT.

Michael Neenan
Windy Dryden

# Acknowledgement

The authors wish to thank the Association for REBT for granting permission to use the following material in modified form in Chapter 2:

Dryden, W. (2002) 'REBT's situational ABC model', *The Rational Emotive Behaviour Therapist*, 10(1): 4–14.

# ONE

## The Distinctive Features of Rational Emotive Behaviour Therapy

We are often asked what are the similarities and differences between rational emotive behaviour therapy (REBT) and cognitive behaviour therapy (CBT). While this seems like a reasonable and straightforward question, we actually find it problematic and difficult to answer. The reason we find the question problematic is this. We consider cognitive behaviour therapy (CBT) to be a therapeutic tradition comprising a number of specific approaches, of which REBT is but one. Thus, when we are asked to compare and contrast REBT with CBT, it is like being asked to compare and contrast an orange (a specific piece of fruit) with fruit (a general category).

Thus, rather than compare REBT (a specific CBT approach) with CBT (a general therapeutic tradition), we prefer to outline what makes REBT distinctive within the CBT tradition. So, in this opening chapter, we will discuss fifteen of REBT's distinctive theoretical features and fifteen of its distinctive practical features. So, when you have read the following thirty distinctive features of REBT, you should have a good idea about what makes REBT distinctive within the therapeutic tradition of CBT. Note that we are not saying that these thirty features are unique to REBT and only to REBT. Rather, we are saying that, taken together, these features outline the distinctiveness of REBT.

Before we undertake our task, it is worth saying that REBT is the oldest of the extant specific CBT approaches, being established by Albert Ellis (1913–2007) in the late 1950s. It is thus over fifty years old, and while it is still developing, what appears in this book are its key ideas described in a nutshell!

# The distinctive theoretical features of REBT

In this section, we will outline REBT's major distinctive theoretical features.

## Postmodern relativism

REBT espouses postmodern relativism, which is antithetical to rigid and extreme views and holds that there is, in all probability, no absolute way of determining reality. Note that we have said 'in all probability' here, for had we said that there is no absolute way of determining reality, then this would have been an absolute statement, antithetical to REBT theory.

## REBT's position on human nature

All approaches to counselling and psychotherapy are based on explicit or implicit ideas about human nature. In selecting a schema to outline REBT's views of human nature we have chosen Hjelle and Ziegler's (1992) 'basic assumptions' approach, which puts forward nine continua on which REBT and other approaches can be located with respect to their position on this issue. We have spelt out this position in Table 1.1.

**Table 1.1** *Description of the nine basic assumptions concerning human nature and REBT's position on these continua*

* **Freedom – Determinism**
How much internal freedom do people have and how much are they determined by external and internal (e.g. biological) factors?
*REBT's position: Moderate emphasis towards the freedom end of the continuum*

* **Rationality – Irrationality**
To what extent are people primarily rational, directing themselves through reason or to what extent are they guided by irrational factors?
*REBT's position: Mid-range between the two. People have the capacity to be both rational and irrational. They have to work harder to be rational than irrational*

**Table 1.1**   (Continued)

- **Holism – Elementalism**

To what extent are people best comprehended as a whole or to what extent by being broken down into their constituent parts?

*REBT's position: Moderate emphasis towards holism end of the continuum*

- **Constitutionalism – Environmentalism**

To what extent are people the result of constitutional factors and to what extent are they products of environmental influences?

*REBT's position: Strong emphasis towards the constitutionalism end of the continuum*

- **Changeability – Unchangeability**

To what extent are people capable of fundamental change over time?

*REBT's position: Moderate emphasis towards the changeability end of the continuum*

- **Subjectivity – Objectivity**

To what extent are people influenced by subjective factors and to what extent by external, objective factors?

*REBT's position: Strong emphasis towards the subjectivity end of the continuum*

- **Proactivity – Reactivity**

To what extent do people generate their behaviour internally (proactivity) and to what extent do they respond to external stimuli (reactivity)?

*REBT's position: Strong emphasis towards the proactivity end of the continuum*

- **Homeostasis – Heterostasis**

To what extent are humans motivated primarily to reduce tensions and maintain an inner homeostasis and to what extent are they motivated to actualize themselves?

*REBT's position: Mid-range between the two*

- **Knowability – Unknowability**

To what extent is human nature fully knowable?

*REBT's position: Moderate emphasis towards the unknowability end of the continuum*

*Source*: Hjelle and Ziegler, 1992

## REBT's distinctive ABC model

Most approaches to CBT outline an 'ABC' meditational model when the person's responses at 'C' to an event at 'A' are mediated by their thoughts and/or beliefs (B) about the event. This view is articulated in Epictetus's oft-quoted dictum: 'Men are disturbed not by things, but by their views of things'. Now, different CBT approaches have different versions of this ABC model and in Chapter 2 we will outline REBT's distinctive 'Situational ABC' model which highlights key inferential aspects of 'A' and argues that 'C' can be emotive, behavioural and cognitive in nature. It also stresses that 'ABCs' are best understood within a situational context.

## Rigidity is at the core of psychological disturbance

REBT argues that a defining characteristic of humans is that we have desires. We want certain things to happen and other things not to happen. However, we also a have a strong tendency to transform these desires into absolute musts, shoulds and oughts, etc. When we hold rigid beliefs of this nature, we disturb ourselves. Thus, in REBT, rigidity is seen as being at the core of psychologically disturbed responses to adversity.

## Flexibility is at the core of psychological health

As we mentioned above, we have desires as humans. However, if we recognize that we don't have to get what we want and we don't have to be spared of what we don't want, we will not disturb ourselves about the adversities that we face. Thus, in REBT, flexibility is seen as being at the core of psychologically healthy responses to adversity.

## Extreme beliefs are derived from rigid beliefs

As we pointed out above, rigid beliefs are at the core of psychologically disturbed responses to adversity. REBT theory also holds that three extreme beliefs are derived from such rigidity in the face of adversity. These are known as: awfulizing beliefs, discomfort intolerance beliefs and depreciation beliefs. We will discuss these in Chapter 2.

## Non-extreme beliefs are derived from flexible beliefs

As we pointed out above, flexible beliefs are at the core of psychologically healthy responses to adversity. REBT theory also holds that three non-extreme beliefs are derived from such rigidity in the face of adversity. These are known as: non-awfulizing beliefs, discomfort tolerance beliefs and acceptance beliefs. We will also discuss these in Chapter 2.

## Distinction between unhealthy negative emotions (UNEs) and healthy negative emotions (HNEs)

As we discussed above, when we face adversity, we have a choice. We can either make ourselves disturbed about this adversity or we can respond in psychologically healthy ways. Depending on what we disturb ourselves about, the emotional component of such disturbance can be expressed in one or more of the following unhealthy negative emotions: anxiety, depression, guilt, shame, hurt, unhealthy anger, unhealthy jealousy and unhealthy envy. These unhealthy negative emotions (or UNEs) are deemed to stem from irrational (i.e. rigid and extreme) beliefs. These UNEs may vary in intensity according to the strength of the person's irrational beliefs.

When we respond healthily to the same adversities, we still experience negative emotions, but these emotions will be healthy in their effects. In REBT, these are known as healthy negative emotions (or HNEs) and are as follows: concern, sadness, remorse, disappointment, healthy anger, healthy jealousy and healthy envy. They are deemed to stem from rational (i.e. flexible and non-extreme) beliefs. These HNEs may also vary in intensity according to the strength of the person's rational beliefs.

## Explaining why clients' inferences are highly distorted

In clinical practice you will encounter situations where your clients will disclose highly distorted inferences (e.g. 'I will become a bag lady'; 'I will lose complete control of myself'; 'I am having a heart attack'). In other approaches to CBT, these tend to be treated as other less highly distorted inferences are and are subject to empirical enquiry. While this can also be done in REBT, in this form of CBT such highly distorted inferences are conceptualized as cognitive consequences of irrational beliefs, and before they are targeted for intervention the irrational beliefs that spawn them are questioned first.

## Position on human worth

REBT has a unique perspective on the issue of human worth, which is particularly relevant to problems of self-esteem (where judgements of the worth of self are salient) and unhealthy anger (where judgements of the worth of others are often made). REBT's view is that as humans are constantly in flux and are highly complex, we cannot legitimately be assigned a single, global judgement or rating that completely accounts for us. Consequently, the REBT alternative is to unconditionally accept humans as fallible, complex and changeable, but to give legitimate evaluations to our rateable aspects (e.g. our behaviour, thoughts, etc.).

REBT's view is that, like self-actualization, unconditional acceptance of self and others is something to strive for, not to attain once and for all.

## Distinction between ego and discomfort disturbance and health

REBT argues that there are two major personal domains in which people experience emotional problems: the ego domain (in which problems revolve around a person's lack of self-esteem) and the discomfort domain (in which problems are about anything else). When Ellis (1979a, 1980a) first introduced this distinction, he was referring to two different types of anxiety: ego anxiety (experienced when the person held an irrational belief about a threat to her self-esteem) and discomfort anxiety (experienced when the person held an irrational belief about a threat to her sense of comfort).

Since then, these terms have been applied much more widely than to anxiety so that when a person holds a demand and self-depreciation belief about an adversity, she is said to experience ego disturbance and when, in the face of the adversity, she holds a demand and any irrational derivative belief other than a self-depreciation belief, she is said to experience discomfort disturbance.

Also, when the person holds a flexible, non-dogmatic preference and a self-acceptance belief in the face of an adversity, the person is said to experience ego health and when she holds a flexible, non-dogmatic preference and any rational derivative belief other than a self-depreciation belief in the face of an adversity, she is said to experience discomfort health.

## Focus on meta-emotional disturbance

While other animals may be said to experience symptoms consistent with psychological disturbance, only we humans appear to have the ability to disturb ourselves about our disturbances. In REBT this is known as meta-emotional disturbance (Dryden, 2009) or secondary disturbance (Walen et al., 1992), and REBT therapists have long since emphasized the early assessment and treatment of this form of disturbance and the need to give clinical priority to it over the person's primary disturbance when its existence impedes the person from dealing effectively with the latter.

## The biological basis of human irrationality

Most other approaches to CBT are based on social learning theories which stress that psychological disturbance occurs as a result of faulty learning. REBT, on the other hand, argues that there is a strong biological basis to psychological disturbance. Thus, for example, independent of their learning history, people seem to find it very easy to transform their preferences into rigid demands, particularly when these preferences are strongly held. They also find it easy to slip back after making psychological advances. While some people think that this view is overly pessimistic, REBT theorists argue that it is realistic. For while people have a strong tendency to irrational thinking, they also have a tendency to rational thinking (Ellis, 1976).

## Choice-based constructivism and going against the grain

This point is actually linked to the previous one, for despite our biological tendencies, we have a choice whether we construct rigid beliefs from our preferences or keep these beliefs flexible by recognizing that we do not have to get what we want. If our rigid beliefs are entrenched, we can still choose to change them by questioning these irrational beliefs and acting and thinking in ways that are consistent with our chosen rational beliefs. However, to do so we need to 'go against the grain' of our irrational beliefs and put up with the discomfort of doing so.

## Position on good mental health

REBT is very explicit about what constitutes good mental health, more explicit in this respect than other CBT therapies. REBT not only sees its aim as the remediation of psychological disturbance, it also strives to help clients to work towards being as psychologically healthy as possible. This is how REBT conceptualizes good mental health. People with good mental health (GMH):

- Take responsibility for their own feelings and behaviour
- Are flexible and non-extreme in their beliefs about self, others and the world
- Value scientific thinking and are non-utopian in outlook
- Adopt an enlightened self-interested position where they look after their own interests, but are mindful of the interests of others and of the environment, sometimes putting the latter two ahead of their own interests
- Are self-directed in orientation rather than relying on others to provide them with direction
- Recognize that happiness stems from making a strong commitment to meaningful pursuits and acing on this commitment
- Take calculated risks to achieve their goals
- Adopt a balance between short-range and long-term hedonism.

# The distinctive practical features of REBT

In this section we will outline REBT's major distinctive practical features.

## The therapeutic relationship in REBT

Like other approaches to CBT, REBT regards the core conditions of empathy, respect and genuineness as highly desirable, but neither necessary nor sufficient to bring about therapeutic change (Ellis, 1994).

REBT offers the following distinctive positions on the therapeutic relationship.

### Therapist warmth

Ellis (in Dryden, 1997) argued that being overly warm runs the risk of reinforcing clients' dire need for approval. Reasonable warmth is advocated instead.

## Therapist acceptance

REBT recommends therapists' showing clients unconditional acceptance rather than respect or prizing (Rogers, 1957) since the danger of
the latter is that it is based on a positive rating that clients can use
conditionally (i.e. 'I am worthwhile because my therapist respects me'
with the implication that I would not be worthwhile if my therapist did
not respect me). Unconditional acceptance teaches the clients that they
can accept themselves whether they are accepted or not, whether by
their therapist or by others.

## Informality

REBT therapists tend towards informality of therapeutic style, although
we can be formal when required. This informality communicates a
number of messages to clients:

- It communicates that REBT therapists take themselves and their role
  seriously, but not too seriously
- It lessens the emotional distance between therapist and client without
  compromising the purpose of therapy
- It communicates therapeutic parity between therapist and client.

## Therapist humour

Therapist humour is emphasized more heavily in REBT than in other
CBT approaches. It is focused on aspects of clients rather than directed
at the clients themselves and, like therapist informality, it communicates
that psychological disturbance results when people take themselves,
other people and/or life conditions not just seriously, but *too* seriously.

## Position on case formulation

In CBT, there is a general agreement on the importance of case formulation. It is seen as providing order to the conceptualization and treatment
of the client's problems and is best done before treatment interventions
are undertaken. REBT's view on this issue is different. We do not routinely wait to intervene on our clients' problems until we have carried

out a case formulation. Rather, we tend to intervene more quickly on a client's target problem and build up a formulation of the 'case' as we go rather than structuring therapy into formulation–intervention stages. We do this because it provides clients with quicker, more efficient help.

Elsewhere, I (WD) have argued that a full case formulation is undertaken before treatment:

- When it is clear that the person has many complex problems
- When resistance occurs in clients who have at first sight non-complex problems and where usual ways of addressing such resistance have proven unsuccessful
- When clients have had several unsuccessful previous attempts at therapy, particularly REBT (Dryden, 1998a).

## Psycho-educational emphasis

REBT has a distinct view on how people disturb themselves, how they perpetuate their disturbance and how they can change. In REBT we are open with our clients about our views and explicitly teach them how to apply REBT concepts in their everyday lives. Of the extant CBT approaches, REBT is the one that has a psycho-educational emphasis that is evident in a variety of therapeutic modalities and self-help materials.

## Dealing with problems in order: disturbance; dissatisfaction; development

People come to therapy with a variety of problems. They are often dissatisfied in areas of their life, they disturb themselves about their dissatisfactions and they fail to develop their personal capacities. As a result, therapists need some schema for dealing with such problems in their logical order. In REBT we argue that the most logical order is as follows:

- We deal with clients' disturbances about their dissatisfactions before dealing with the dissatisfactions themselves. We do this because as long as clients are disturbed about their dissatisfactions, their disturbances will prevent them from dealing effectively with these areas of dissatisfaction.

- Once we have helped clients deal with their disturbed feelings about their dissatisfactions, we help them deal with these dissatisfactions before we help them to deal with developing their personal capacities. We do this because as long as clients are preoccupied with life's dissatisfactions they won't be able to give their full attention to issues of personal development.

## Early focus on irrational beliefs

As we have seen, REBT theory holds that people disturb themselves about life's adversities because they hold irrational beliefs about these adversities. As such, the best way we can help our clients is to help them to change their irrational beliefs to rational beliefs. Consequently, REBT therapists use the automatic thoughts and distorted inferences that clients disclose as a way of helping them as quickly as possible to identify and change the irrational beliefs that spawn these other cognitions. So, REBT advocates an early focus on irrational cognitive schemas whereas other approaches to CBT will tend to focus on more surface cognitions before dealing with underlying schemas.

## Helping clients to change their irrational beliefs to rational beliefs

Perhaps the most distinctive feature about REBT practice is the efforts that REBT therapists make to help clients change their irrational (rigid and extreme) beliefs to rational (flexible and non-extreme) beliefs. This process involves a number of steps:

- Helping clients to *detect* their irrational beliefs
- Helping clients to *discriminate* their irrational beliefs from their rational belief alternatives
- Helping clients to *dispute* their irrational and rational beliefs
- Helping clients to strengthen their conviction in their rational beliefs and weaken their conviction in their irrational beliefs.

We discuss this in greater detail in Chapters 2, 3 and 4.

# Use of logical arguments in disputing beliefs

DiGiuseppe (1991) has argued that REBT therapists employ three major arguments when questioning or disputing their clients' beliefs (both irrational and rational). These are:

- Empirical arguments (e.g. 'Is your demand consistent with reality?')
- Logical arguments (e.g. 'Does it logically follow that you can rate your whole self on the basis of a part of yourself?')
- Pragmatic arguments (e.g. 'What are the consequences of your discomfort intolerance belief?').

Most CBT approaches employ empirical and pragmatic arguments, but place little emphasis on logical questioning. In REBT we use all three. We do realize that most clients may find logical arguments less persuasive than the other two arguments, but some clients do find logical arguments convincing. Given that the best way of knowing to which arguments clients best resonate is to use them and observe their effects, REBT therapists will give all three equal weight and stick with arguments that clients find most useful.

# Variety of therapeutic styles

CBT therapists all tend to take a broad active-directive style to therapy. Indeed, it would be difficult to practise CBT passively and without any direction. Also, if CBT therapists were not allowed to ask questions in therapy they would soon flounder. Having said that, REBT therapists tend to use a broader range of styles than other CBT therapists. Thus, in general, we can practise REBT, formally or informally, seriously or with humour.

When it comes to disputing beliefs we can use the following styles:

- A *Socratic style* where therapists ask clients open-ended questions designed to encourage them to see for themselves that their irrational beliefs are irrational and that rational beliefs are rational and the reasons why this is the case
- A *didactic style* where therapists didactically teach clients the same thing, ensuring that clients understand the didactic points being made

- A *metaphorical style* where therapists adopt a metaphorical stance and tell stories designed to illustrate the irrationality of irrational beliefs and the rationality of rational beliefs
- A *humorous style* where therapists use humour to encourage clients to see how ridiculous their irrational ideas are
- An *enactive style* where therapists use action in the therapy setting to illustrate the irrationality of irrational ideas.

Whichever styles therapists employ it is important that the working alliance between therapist and client is preserved and that the therapist is genuine in using the style. Lazarus (1981) has remarked that effective therapists are authentic chameleons in varying therapeutic styles and this is certainly the case in REBT.

## Discourages gradualism

In order to benefit effectively from REBT, clients need to confront their adversities at 'A' while rehearsing their rational beliefs at 'B', while ensuring that their behaviour and thinking at 'C' are consistent with their rational thinking. Clients who fully confront their adversities in this way will get the most out of REBT, but quite often they find doing so 'too much' for them. In such cases, they can either confront their adversities in a very gradual manner or they can use the 'challenging, but not overwhelming' principle (Dryden, 1985), where they take steps that are challenging to them, but not overwhelming to them at the time. While REBT therapists would prefer their clients to use full exposure, they are keen to discourage them from proceeding very gradually, since doing so reinforces their discomfort intolerance beliefs.

## Change is hard work, and the use of force and energy

In an ideal world therapeutic change would be quick and easy. In the real world, however, it is hard work and involves repeated and forceful 'going against the irrational grain'. For this reason, REBT therapists use a forceful approach with their clients when appropriate, but in ways that preserve the working alliance between them and their clients. They also encourage their clients to be forceful with themselves (Ellis, 1979b).

## Emphasis on teaching clients general rational philosophies and encouraging them to make a profound philosophic change

As we pointed out above, REBT therapists are interested not only in helping their clients address their disturbances and dissatisfactions, they are also keen to help them, if required, to develop their personal capacities. As part of this part of their work, they can offer their clients an opportunity to develop general philosophies that, if adopted and implemented, can help clients become, in Ellis's memorable (1999) phrase, 'less disturbable'. If clients are able and willing to make a 'profound philosophic change', they work towards developing a set of flexible, non-awfulizing, discomfort tolerance and acceptance beliefs about what happens to them, their loved ones and the larger social and physical world.

We should stress, however, that most clients are not interested in developing such a general rational philosophy and for those who are it is a lifetime's work. Like self-actualization, it is a state to strive for and can never be attained perfectly and once and for all. Nevertheless, REBT is unique among CBT approaches in offering clients such an opportunity and is clear about how interested clients can go about doing this.

## Compromises in therapeutic change

As we have seen, REBT argues that changing their beliefs is the most profound and enduring way in which clients can help themselves deal effectively with their emotional problems. REBT recognizes, however, that clients may not be able or willing to change their irrational beliefs and in such cases it recommends making compromises with the ideal of belief change. In such cases, we can help our clients:

- Achieve inferential change by encouraging them to question and re-think their distorted inferences so that they view events more realistically
- Achieve behavioural change by helping them to respond to adversities more effectively

- Achieve situational change by encouraging them to change the situation in which the adversity occurred if it can be changed or to remove themselves from the situation if it can't be changed.

It may be that once clients have made these other changes, they may be open to changing their irrational beliefs to rational ones.

## Focus on clients' misconceptions, doubts, reservations and objections to REBT

As we mentioned earlier, REBT has a decided psycho-educational focus and believes that people can be taught the principles of rational thinking and healthy living, at least from the perspective of REBT. As these concepts are explicitly discussed with clients, it happens that they may develop doubts, reservations and objections to REBT concepts and ideas (Dryden, 2001). For example, some people are reluctant to change their rigid musts, because they think that they need these to motivate them to take action. Many such doubts etc. held by clients are based on misconceptions of rational concepts and when these are identified by the therapist, he or she engages the client in a productive dialogue about the basis of the misconception.

An important skill that effective REBT therapists have is to identify the presence of clients' doubts when they are implicitly rather than explicitly communicated. Unless this is done the client will be guided by the doubt and this will serve as an obstacle to change.

## Therapeutic efficiency

A distinctive feature of REBT is the emphasis it places on efficiency in its practice. In a seminal paper, Ellis (1980b) specified several criteria of psychotherapeutic efficiency. None of these criteria on its own defines REBT's distinctive contribution. This is defined by all seven in concert. These are:

- **Brevity:** Helping clients in as short a time as possible
- **Depth-centredness:** Helping clients by focusing at the deep level of irrational beliefs and encouraging them to change these to rational beliefs
- **Pervasiveness:** Helping clients to deal with many of their problems, rather than with a few presenting symptoms

- **Extensiveness:** Helping clients not only to minimize their disturbed feelings, but also to promote their potential for happy living
- **Thoroughgoingness:** Helping clients by using a plethora of cognitive, emotive and behavioural techniques in a thoroughgoing manner
- **Maintaining therapeutic progress:** Helping clients maintain their progress and deal with vulnerable factors that would otherwise lead to lapses and relapse
- **Promotion of prevention:** Helping clients to prevent the development of new problems in the future.

The above ways of working are offered to clients, not foisted on them.

## Theoretically consistent eclecticism

REBT is a form of theoretically consistent eclecticism (Dryden, 1986), meaning that it advocates the broad use of techniques, from wherever, but to achieve goals in keeping with REBT theory. For example, when an REBT therapist employs the two-chair technique that originates from gestalt therapy, it is to help the client to identify an irrational belief or as a disputing technique designed to encourage a dialogue between the irrational and rational parts of his mind; it is not to resolve splits in the person's psyche, as it would be in gestalt therapy (Passons, 1975).

REBT also specifies techniques that it recommends its practitioners to avoid using (although not in an absolute sense). These are techniques that may reinforce rather than tackle a person's irrational beliefs (e.g. gradual desensitization with clients who have discomfort intolerance beliefs and being overly warm with clients who have a dire need for approval).

## Chapter summary

In this opening chapter we have made the point that to compare and contrast REBT (a specific approach) with CBT (a general therapeutic tradition) is not meaningful. Rather, it is more accurate to consider REBT's distinctive theoretical and practical features, which we have listed here. If you are interested in reading more on this subject, we suggest that you look at Dryden (2009).

We are now ready to consider REBT's ABC framework in greater detail, which we do in Chapter 2.

# TWO

# The REBT 'Situational ABC' Model

## Introduction

In this chapter we will present a situational version of REBT's 'ABC' model. Traditionally 'A' has stood for an activating event, literally an event that activates the person's beliefs at 'B'. 'C' stands for the consequences that the person experiences when holding these beliefs about the activating event. There have been many versions of REBT's 'ABC' model (e.g. Grieger & Boyd, 1980; Walen et al., 1992; Wessler & Wessler, 1980; Woods, 1991) and before we present our situational version of the model in detail, let us summarize its main features.

- It roots the 'ABC' components in a specific situational context, thus underscoring that people tend to disturb themselves most in specific situational contexts.
- It puts forward the view that the 'A' that triggers 'B' is best described as the 'critical A'.
- It thus distinguishes between a 'critical A' and the situation in which the 'critical A' occurs.
- It makes clear that 'Cs' can be emotional, behavioural and cognitive in nature.
- It is very explicit in differentiating rational beliefs from irrational beliefs by making clear the different components of each.
- It does not intend to be comprehensive and thus, for example, does not deal with core irrational beliefs and their core rational equivalents. It does not do so because these core beliefs are general in nature and span different situational contexts.

## Overview

We will briefly describe the model in basic form before discussing each element in greater detail.

### 'Situation'

As humans, we do not react in a vacuum. Rather, we think, feel and act in specific situations. The term 'situation' in the context of the 'Situational ABC' model refers to a descriptive account of the actual event in which our response occurs.

### 'A' = critical activating event

Within this specific 'situation', when we have a significant emotional reaction it is usually to a key or critical aspect of this 'situation'. This is known as the critical activating event (henceforth known as the 'critical A'). Sometimes 'A' has been called an 'adversity' when it is negative.

### 'B' = belief

It is a major premise of REBT that while our emotions are usually about a 'critical A', this 'A' does not cause our emotional reaction. Rather, our emotions are primarily determined by the beliefs (at 'B') that we hold about the 'critical A'.

### 'C' = consequences of the beliefs at 'B' about the 'critical A'

Thus, when your client holds a belief about a 'critical A', he will tend to experience an emotion, he will tend to act in a certain way and he will tend to think in certain ways. These three consequences of this 'A' × 'B' interaction are known as emotional, behavioural and thinking consequences, respectively.

Let us now discuss each of these elements in greater detail.

# 'Situation'

As we said earlier, emotional episodes do not take place in a vacuum; rather they occur in specific 'situations'. Such 'situations' are viewed in the 'Situational ABC' model as descriptions of actual events about which your client forms inferences (see below). 'Situations' exist in time. Thus, they can describe past actual events (e.g. 'My boss asked me to see him at the end of the day'), present actual events (e.g. 'My boss is asking me to see him at the end of the day') or future events (e.g. 'My boss will ask me to see him at the end of the day'). Note that we have not referred to such future events as future actual events since we do not know that such events will occur and this is why such future events may prove to be false. But if we look at such future 'situations', they are still descriptions of what may happen and do not add inferential meaning (see below).

'Situations' may refer to internal actual events (i.e. events that occur within ourselves, e.g. thoughts, feelings, bodily sensations, aches and pains, etc.) or to external actual events (i.e. events that occur outside ourselves, e.g. your client's boss asking to see her). Their defining characteristic is as before: they are descriptions of events and do not include inferential meaning.

# 'A'

As we said above, 'A' stands for a critical activating event and is the aspect of the 'situation' about which your client experiences an emotional reaction. As we will show below, there are other aspects of the 'situation' to which your client does not respond emotionally and these are known as 'non-critical As'. Given this, when we mention 'A' we refer to a 'critical A' unless otherwise specified.

Let us make a number of points about 'A'.

## 'A' is usually an inference

'A' is usually an inference and needs to be differentiated from the 'situation' or actual event about which it is made. An inference is basically an interpretation or hunch about the 'situation', whereas the 'situation' is purely descriptive. Let us provide you with an example to make this distinction clear.

Imagine that your client receives a message from her boss to the effect that he wants to see her at the end of the day. She has an emotional response about this and thinks that him wanting to see her means that he is going to criticize her work. Here we have:

'Situation' (or actual event) = 'My boss wants to see me at the end of the day'

'Critical A' = 'My boss is going to criticize my work'

As can be seen from this example, the 'situation' is a description of the facts of the matter whereas the 'A' is a critical or key inference that your client has made about the 'situation'. The 'A' is critical because it is the aspect of the 'situation' to which your client has an emotional response. When your client has a significant emotional response to an event or 'situation', the 'A' represents the personalized inferential meaning that she has given to the 'situation'.

## The 'critical A' can be true or false

Inferences that usually comprise the 'critical A' can be true or false and as such when your client makes such an inference she needs to evaluate it against the available evidence.

In the above example, it may be true that your client's boss is going to criticize her work when she goes to see him at the end of the working day or it may be false. All she can do is to consider the available evidence and come up with the 'best bet' about what is going to happen at the meeting with the boss. This involves considering such factors as: (a) what has happened in the past when her boss has asked to see her; (b) the quality of the work that she recently submitted to her boss; and (c) how judgemental or otherwise her boss is in general.

## The 'critical A' can also be about a past, present or future event

Your client's 'critical A' can be about a past, present or future 'situation' or actual event, and when it is she gives that event inferential meaning. Thus:

Past 'situation' = 'My boyfriend did not return my call'

'Critical A' about past 'situation' = 'This proves that he doesn't care for me'

Present 'situation' = 'My father is discussing the value of saving regularly'

'Critical A' about present 'situation' = 'My father is criticizing me for over-spending '

Future 'situation' = 'The hospital will contact me with the results of my blood test'

'Critical A' about future 'situation' = 'The blood test will show that I am ill'

## A 'critical A' can be about an external event or an internal event

The defining characteristic of this 'critical A' is again its inferential nature. For example:

External 'situation' = Letter with a cheque in it has gone missing

'Critical A' about external 'situation' = 'Somebody has stolen my cheque'

Internal 'situation' = Intrusive thought about hitting someone

'Critical A' about internal 'situation' = 'I am losing control'

## 'Non-critical As'

In any given 'situation', it is possible to make alternative inferences. We call such inferences 'non-critical As'. For example, in the 'situation' in which your client's boss wishes to see her at the end of the day, it is possible that he wants to commend her on her work or he may wish to speak about a future meeting that they both have and not about her work. These are just two possible 'non-critical As'. These inferences are non-critical because your client has not made them and they are not associated with her emotional response.

'Situation' (or actual event) = 'My boss wants to see me at the end of the day'

'Critical A' = 'My boss is going to criticize my work.'

'Non-critical A' Number 1 = 'My boss is going to commend me on my work'

'Non-critical 'A' Number 2 = 'My boss wants to discuss a future meeting that we both have'

However, if she rethinks the 'situation' and concludes that her boss does want to commend her work and not criticize it and she has a new emotional response to the being commended 'situation', this previously 'non-critical A' becomes her new 'critical A' and her previous 'critical A' becomes non-critical.

## 'B'

Beliefs are attitudes that can be rational (or healthy) or irrational (or unhealthy). You can hold beliefs about descriptive 'situations', but more often you will hold beliefs about the critical 'As' that you make about this more objective 'situation'. In this section, we will be using some technical language. We wish to make it clear at the outset that we use such language to help you understand professional concepts. We suggest that you do not use such language with your clients as you will be likely to confuse them if you do.

## Rational beliefs

REBT argues that there are four basic rational beliefs, which have the following five major characteristics:

- Flexible or non-extreme
- Conducive to your mental health
- Helpful to you as you strive towards your goals
- True
- Logical.

Now let us discuss the four rational beliefs put forward by REBT theory. These are:

Non-dogmatic preference                    (Flexible belief)

Non-awfulizing belief                      (Non-extreme belief)
Discomfort tolerance belief                (Non-extreme belief)
Acceptance belief                          (Non-extreme belief)

You will recall from Chapter 1 (see pp. 4–5) that according to REBT theory, a flexible belief (i.e. non-dogmatic preference) is at the very core of a client's healthy response to an adversity at 'A' and the three non-extreme beliefs (listed above) are derived from this flexible belief. This is shown in the diagram above. We will now discuss the four rational beliefs in turn.

### Non-dogmatic preference

Human beings have desires, and for desires to be the cornerstone of healthy functioning they take the form of a non-dogmatic preference. This has two components. The first component is called the 'asserted preference' component. Here, your client makes clear to herself what she wants (either what she wants to happen or exist or what she does not want to happen or exist). The second component is called the 'negated demand' component. Here, your client acknowledges that she does not have to have her desires met.

In short, we have:

Non-dogmatic preference = 'Asserted preference' component + 'Negated demand' component

Using the example that we introduced above, if your client holds a non-dogmatic preference about her 'critical A', we have:

'Situation' = 'My boss wants to see me at the end of the day'

'Critical A' = 'My boss is going to criticize my work'

'Asserted preference' component = 'I don't want my boss to criticize my work …'

'Negated demand' component = '… but he does not have to do what I want him to do'

Non-dogmatic preference = 'I don't want my boss to criticize my work, but he does not have to do what I want him to do'

## Non-awfulizing belief

When your client's non-dogmatic preference is not met it is healthy for her to conclude that it is bad that she has not got what she wanted. It is not healthy for her to be indifferent about not getting what she desires. As with a non-dogmatic preference, a non-awfulizing belief has two components. The first component is called the 'asserted badness' component. Here, your client acknowledges that it is bad that she has not got what she wants or that she has got what she doesn't want. The second component is called the 'negated awfulizing' component. Here, your client acknowledges that while it is bad when she doesn't get her desires met, it is not awful, terrible or the end of the world when this happens.

In short, we have:

Non-awfulizing belief = 'Asserted badness' component + 'Negated awfulizing' component

Using the example that we introduced above, if your client holds a non-dogmatic preference about her 'critical A', her non-awfulizing belief will be as follows:

'Situation' = 'My boss wants to see me at the end of the day'

'Critical A' = 'My boss is going to criticize my work'

'Asserted badness' component = 'It would bad if my boss criticizes my work ...'

'Negated awfulizing' component = '... but not terrible if he does'

Non-awfulizing belief = 'It would be bad if my boss criticizes my work, but not terrible if he does'

## Discomfort tolerance belief

When your client's non-dogmatic preference is not met it is healthy for her to conclude that it is difficult for her to tolerate not getting what she wants, but that she can tolerate it. A discomfort tolerance belief has three components. The first component is called the 'asserted struggle' component because your client recognizes that it is a struggle to put up with not getting what she wants. The second component is called the 'negated unbearability' component. Here, your client acknowledges that while it is a struggle to tolerate not getting her desires met it is not intolerable. The third component is called the 'worth tolerating' component and points to the fact that not only can your client tolerate not getting what she wants, it is also worth it to her to do so.

In short, we have:

Discomfort tolerance belief = 'Asserted struggle' component + 'Negated unbearability' component + 'Worth tolerating' component

Using the example that we introduced above, if your client holds a non-dogmatic preference about her 'critical A', her discomfort tolerance belief will be as follows:

'Situation' = 'My boss wants to see me at the end of the day'

'Critical A' = 'My boss is going to criticize my work'

'Asserted struggle' component = 'It would be hard to put up with if my boss criticizes my work …'

'Negated unbearability' component = '… but it would not be unbearable if he does. I can bear it …'

'Worth tolerating' component = '… and it is worth it to me to do so'

Discomfort tolerance belief = 'It would be hard to put up with if my boss criticizes my work, but it would not be unbearable if he does. I can bear it and it is worth it for me to do so'

## Acceptance belief

When your client's non-dogmatic preference is not met it is healthy for her to accept this state of affairs. There are three types of acceptance belief: a self-acceptance belief, where your client accepts herself for not meeting her desires or for not having them met; an other-acceptance belief, where your client accepts another person or other people for not meeting her desires; and an acceptance of life conditions belief, where she accepts life conditions when they don't meet her desires.

There are three components to an acceptance belief, which we will illustrate with reference to a self-acceptance belief. The first component is called the 'negatively evaluated aspect' component. Here, your client recognizes when she has not met her desires or when her desires have not been met by others or by life conditions and she evaluates this particular aspect negatively. The second component is called the 'negated global negative evaluation' component. Here, your client acknowledges that while she may have acted badly, for example, or experienced a bad event, the whole of her 'self' is not bad. The third component is called the 'asserted complex fallibility' component. Whereas in the second component your client negated the view that she is a bad person, for example, here she asserts what she is: a complex fallible human being.

In short, we have:

Acceptance belief = 'Negatively evaluated aspect' component + 'Negated global negative evaluation' component + 'Asserted complex fallibility' component

Using the example that we introduced above, if your client holds a non-dogmatic preference about her 'critical A', her self-acceptance belief (in this instance) will be as follows:

'Situation' = 'My boss wants to see me at the end of the day'

'Critical A' = 'My boss is going to criticize my work'

'Negatively evaluated aspect' component = 'It would be bad if my boss criticizes my work ...'

'Negated global negative evaluation' component = '... but it would not prove that I am worthless ...'

'Asserted complex fallibility' component = '... Rather, I am a complex, fallible human being and this does not change no matter what my boss thinks of my work'

Self-acceptance belief = 'It would be bad if my boss criticizes my work, but it would not prove that I am worthless. Rather, I am a complex, fallible human being and this does not change no matter what my boss thinks of my work'

Before we go on to consider irrational beliefs from an REBT perspective, let us reiterate a point we made earlier in the chapter. We have taken great care to outline the components of the rational beliefs presented here and we have given these components their complex professional terms. When you develop rational beliefs with your clients, you should be guided by these components, but what is more important is that you develop rational beliefs that are clear, simple and easy to remember. This is a skill that does depend on a thorough understanding of the more formal constituents of these beliefs.

## Irrational beliefs

REBT argues that there are four basic irrational beliefs which have the following five major characteristics:

- Rigid or extreme
- Conducive to psychological disturbance
- Unhelpful to you as you strive towards your goals
- False
- Illogical.

Now let us discuss the four irrational beliefs put forward by REBT theory. These are:

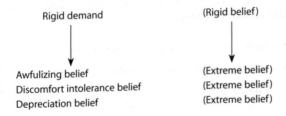

You will again recall from Chapter 1 (see pp. 4–5) that according to REBT theory, a rigid belief (i.e. rigid demand) is at the very core of a client's' unhealthy response to an adversity at 'A' and the three extreme beliefs (listed above) are derived from this rigid belief. This is shown in the diagram above. We will now discuss the four irrational beliefs in turn.

## Rigid demand

REBT theory holds that when your client takes her desires and turns them into rigid demands, absolute necessities, musts, absolute shoulds and the like, she makes herself emotionally disturbed when she does not get what she believes she must get. Even when she does get what she believes she must, she is still vulnerable to emotional disturbance when she holds a rigid demand at the point when she becomes aware that she might lose what she has and must retain.

A rigid demand has two components. The first is known as the 'asserted preference' component and is the same as the 'asserted preference' component of a non-dogmatic preference. Again, your client makes clear to herself what she wants (either what she wants to happen or exist or what she wants not to happen or exist). The second component is called the 'asserted demand' component. Here, your client takes what she wants and transforms it into a 'rigid demand' (e.g. 'I want to do well in my examination and therefore I have to do so').

In short, we have:

Rigid demand = 'Asserted preference' component + 'Asserted demand' component

Using the example that we introduced above, if your client holds a rigid demand 'critical A', we have:

'Situation' = 'My boss wants to see me at the end of the day'

'Critical A' = 'My boss is going to criticize my work'

'Asserted preference' component = 'I don't want my boss to criticize my work …'

'Asserted demand' component = '… and therefore he must not do so'

Demand = 'I don't want my boss to criticize my work and therefore he must not do so'

or

'My boss must not criticize my work'

You will see from the above that we have provided two versions of the client's demand. Please note that the shorter form (i.e. 'My boss must not criticize my work') is the more frequently used by clients, but it is sometimes useful to use the longer form, particularly if you want to show your client how she transforms her desire into a demand.

## Awfulizing belief

When your client's rigid demand is not met then she will tend to make the extreme conclusion that it is awful, horrible, terrible or the end of the world that she hasn't got what she insists she must have. As with a non-awfulizing belief, an awfulizing belief has two components. The first component is the same as that in the non-awfulizing belief – the 'asserted badness' component. Here, you will recall your client acknowledges that it is bad that she has not got what she wants or that she has got what she doesn't want. The second component is called the 'asserted awfulizing' component. Here, your client transforms her non-extreme evaluation of badness into an extreme evaluation of horror (e.g. 'Because it would be bad if I were to fail my exam, it would be horrible were I to do so').

In short, we have:

Awfulizing belief = 'Asserted badness' component + 'Asserted awfulizing' component

Using the example that we introduced above, if your client holds a rigid demand about her 'critical A', her awfulizing belief will be as follows:

'Situation' = 'My boss wants to see me at the end of the day'

'Critical A' = 'My boss is going to criticize my work'

'Asserted badness' component = 'It would be bad if my boss criticizes my work ...'

'Asserted awfulizing' component = '... and therefore it would be terrible if he does'

Awfulizing belief = 'It would be bad if my boss criticizes my work and therefore it would be terrible if he does'

or

'It would be terrible if my boss criticizes my work'

You will again see from the above that we have provided two versions of the client's awfulizing belief. Please note that the shorter form (i.e. 'It would be terrible if my boss criticizes my work') is the more frequently used by clients, but it is sometimes useful to use the longer form, particularly if you want to show your client how she transforms badness into horror.

## Discomfort intolerance belief

When your client's rigid demand is not met, she will tend to make the extreme conclusion that she cannot bear not getting what she demands. Unlike a discomfort tolerance belief, which has three components, a discomfort intolerance belief tends to have only two components. The first component is again known as the 'asserted struggle' component because your client recognizes that it is a struggle to put up with not getting what she believes she must. The second component is called the 'asserted unbearability' component. Here, your client acknowledges that it is not just a struggle to put up with not getting her demand met, it is also intolerable. Since she thinks that she cannot put up with not getting what she demands the issue of whether or not it is worth tolerating this does not become an issue. She believes she can't tolerate it and that's that.

In short, we have:

Discomfort intolerance belief = 'Asserted struggle' component + 'Asserted unbearability' component

Using the example that we introduced above, if your client holds a rigid demand about her 'critical A', her discomfort intolerance belief will be as follows:

'Situation' = 'My boss wants to see me at the end of the day'

'Critical A' = 'My boss is going to criticize my work'

'Asserted struggle' component = 'It would be hard to put up with if my boss criticizes my work ...'

'Asserted unbearability' component = '... and therefore it would be unbearable if he does'

Discomfort intolerance belief = 'It would be hard to put up with if my boss criticizes my work and therefore it would be unbearable if he does'

or

'It would be unbearable if my boss criticizes my work'

Once again you will see from the above that we have provided two versions of the client's discomfort intolerance belief. Please note that the shorter form (i.e. 'It would be unbearble if my boss criticizes my work') is the more frequently used by clients, but it is sometimes useful to use the longer form, particularly if you want to show your client how she transforms struggle into unbearability.

## Depreciation belief

When your client's rigid demand is not met she will tend to depreciate herself, depreciate others or depreciate life conditions. Thus, there are three types of depreciation belief: a self-depreciation belief, where your client depreciates herself for not meeting her demands or for not having them met; an other-depreciation belief, where your client depreciates another person or other people for not meeting her demands; and a depreciation of life conditions belief, where your client depreciates life conditions when they don't meet her demands.

There are two components to a depreciation belief, which we will illustrate with reference to a self-depreciation belief. The first component is called the 'negatively evaluated aspect' component, which is also featured in a self-acceptance belief. Here, your client recognizes when she has not met her demands or that her demands have not been met by others or by life conditions and she evaluates this particular aspect negatively. The second component is called the 'asserted global negative evaluation' component. Here, your client gives herself a global negative rating for not meeting her demands, for example. Thus, she may acknowledge that she has acted badly and then evaluates herself as a bad person for acting badly.

In short, we have:

Depreciation belief = 'Negatively evaluated aspect' component + 'Asserted global negative evaluation' component

Using the example that we introduced above, if your client holds a rigid demand about her 'critical A', her self-depreciation belief (in this instance) will be as follows:

'Situation' = 'My boss wants to see me at the end of the day'

'Critical A' = 'My boss is going to criticize my work'

'Negatively evaluated aspect' component = 'It would be bad if my boss criticizes my work …'

'Asserted global negative evaluation' component = '… and therefore it would prove that I am worthless if he does'

Self-depreciation belief = 'It would be bad if my boss criticizes my work and therefore it would prove that I am worthless if he does'

or

'If my boss criticizes my work, it would prove I am worthless'

For the final time, you will see from the above that we have provided two versions of the client's self-depreciation belief. Please note that the shorter form (i.e. 'If my boss criticizes my work, it would prove I am worthless') is the one more frequently used by clients, but it is sometimes useful to use the longer form, particularly if you want to show your client how she transforms what happens to her into her own worthlessness.

## 'C'

'C' stands for the consequences that your client experiences when she holds a belief at 'B' about 'A'. There are three major consequences which we will consider separately, but which in reality occur together.

## Emotional 'Cs'

When your client's critical 'A' is negative and she holds a set of rational beliefs at 'B' about this 'A', her emotional 'C' will be negative but healthy. Yes, that's right; negative emotions can be healthy. Thus, when your client faces a threat, it is healthy for her to feel concerned and when she has experienced a loss, it is healthy for her to feel sad. Other healthy negative emotions (so called because they feel unpleasant but help clients deal constructively with negative life events) are: remorse, disappointment, sorrow, healthy anger, healthy jealousy and healthy envy.

When your client's critical 'A' is negative, but this time she holds a set of irrational beliefs at 'B' about this 'A', her emotional 'C' will be negative and unhealthy. Thus, when your client faces a threat, it is unhealthy for her to feel anxious and when she has experienced a loss, it is unhealthy for her to feel depressed. Other unhealthy negative emotions (so called because they feel unpleasant and they interfere with clients' dealing constructively with negative life events) are: guilt, shame, hurt, unhealthy anger, unhealthy jealousy and unhealthy envy.

## Behavioural 'Cs'

When your client's critical 'A' is negative and she holds a set of rational beliefs at 'B' about this 'A', her behavioural 'C' is likely to be constructive. Such behaviour is constructive in three ways. First, it will help your client to change the negative event that she is facing if it can be changed. Second, it will help her to make a healthy adjustment if the event cannot be changed. Third, it will help her to go forward and make progress at achieving her goals.

When your client's critical 'A' is negative, but this time she holds a set of irrational beliefs at 'B' about this 'A', her behavioural 'C' is likely to be unconstructive. Such behaviour is unconstructive in three ways. First, it won't help your client to change the negative event that she is facing if it can be changed. Indeed, such unconstructive behaviour will often make a bad situation worse. Second, it will prevent her from making a healthy adjustment if the event cannot be changed. Third, it will take her away from pursuing her goals.

It is important for you to realize that behavioural Cs can be either overt actions or action tendencies that are not converted into actual behaviour. Thus, when you ask your client what she did in a particular situation and she replies that she did not do anything, it is worthwhile to enquire what she felt like doing but which she suppressed.

# Thinking 'Cs'

When your client's critical 'A' is negative and she holds a set of rational beliefs at 'B' about this 'A' her subsequent thinking (or thinking 'C') is likely to be constructive. Such thinking is constructive in two ways. First, it is realistic and allows her to entertain probable rather than unlikely, but highly negative, outcomes. Second, it is balanced and recognizes, for example, that she will get a range of positive, neutral and negative responses to her behaviour. As a result, these thinking 'Cs' enable your client to respond constructively to realistically perceived situations.

When your client's critical 'A' is negative, but this time she holds a set of irrational beliefs at 'B' about this 'A', her subsequent thinking (or thinking 'C') is likely to be unconstructive. Such thinking is unconstructive in two ways. First, it is unrealistic in that she will tend to over-predict the occurrence of low probability, highly aversive outcomes. Second, it is skewed in that she thinks, for example, that most people will respond to her negatively, a few may respond to her neutrally but nobody will respond to her positively. As a result, these thinking 'Cs' interfere with her ability to respond constructively to realistically perceived situations.

Other approaches to CBT (particularly Beck's model) place a lot of attention on cognitive distortions, which from an REBT perspective we see as highly distorted inferences that are best conceptualized as thinking consequences of irrational beliefs. In Appendix 1, we present a list of such distortions and show how they stem from irrational beliefs. In addition, in the same appendix we present a list of realistic and balanced alternatives to these distortions and show how they stem from rational beliefs.

## Chapter summary

In this chapter, we presented REBT's 'Situational ABC' model and showed that when your client holds a set of irrational beliefs about an adversity she makes herself psychologically disturbed. However, when she holds a set of rational beliefs about the same adversity, she reacts to it healthily.

# THREE

## Assessment

In REBT, therapists try to gain, as early as possible, an ABC understanding of the client's presenting problem rather than carry out a pre-treatment case formulation (see Chapter 1, pp. 10–11). Gaining further information, both current and historical, about the problem can be obtained as therapy proceeds. Trying to know the 'big picture' (Grieger and Boyd, 1980), that is, attempting to understand every aspect of the client's functioning before clinical intervention begins, can waste valuable therapy time, prolong the client's distress and convey to her that you are more interested in completing your paperwork than helping her.

## Explaining REBT

REBT is based on the principle of informed consent and this means that you need to explain REBT at the outset to ensure that your client is informed about the approach and can then consent to going forward. When you do this, ensure that your explanation of REBT is brief and clear, not lengthy and elaborate. Initially, the most important initial point to make is the thought–feeling link rather than an explanation of the role of rigid beliefs in emotional disturbance, which will come later. Here are some ways of teaching this link.

### Approach 1: a written example

First, write The 'Situational ABC' model on a piece of paper or whiteboard. Then say:

In this model, the 'situation' is that a person is preparing to take an exam and at 'A' she thinks she may fail the exam. At 'C', emotional consequences, she is feeling very anxious. At 'B', beliefs, she thinks, 'If I don't pass this exam, I'll be an utter failure.' In order to really understand what determines the person's anxiety at 'C', we need to focus on 'B', not 'A'. We will be using this 'ABC' model to understand and examine your emotional problems.

Alternatively, you can be Socratic and ask your client what largely determines 'C' – 'B' or 'A'? – and explore the reasons for her answer.

## Approach 2: tapping the forehead

You can say the following:

Many people believe that their emotional problems are caused by others or unpleasant events in their life. Not so. REBT's position is that our emotional problems are largely self-created through the beliefs and attitudes that we hold [*tapping forehead*]. If you want to change the way you feel about events in your life, you first have to change the way you think about these events. Let's see how REBT can be applied to your problems.

## Approach 3: a very brief explanation

With some clients you might be able to be even more brief:

The essence of REBT is that you feel as you think, so let's see how this principle applies in practice to your problem of … [for example, anxiety].

## Approach 4: focus on meaning

Three men working for the same company, at the same level and on the same salary, are all sacked at the same time. The first man feels depressed because he believes he is worthless without a role in life; the second man feels angry because he believes he should have been promoted, not sacked; and the third man feels relieved because he never liked the job and can set up his own business now. The point is that being sacked does not cause each man's emotional reaction but what does cause it is the *meaning* each man attaches to being sacked. We'll be examining the meaning you attach to events in your life in order to understand your emotional problems.[1]

You can be Socratic instead of telling your client what the point of the story is and ask her what she thinks caused three different emotional reactions to the same event.

Of course, some, or many, of your clients will have doubts, reservations or objections to the thought–feeling link (for example, 'Being sacked makes you depressed because if you got your job back then you would be happy again. That makes sense, doesn't it?'). To avoid prolonged discussion and thereby delay a problem assessment, it is probably best to suggest to your clients that doubts, reservations and objections can be dealt with by showing REBT in action (unless your client insists on discussing the ABC model before therapy proceeds any further).

## Listening to clients' stories

Obviously clients come to therapy with a story to tell about their problems. For REBT therapists, the concern is when to intervene in this

---

[1] In classical REBT, these three men are facing different 'critical As': loss of role (man 1), unfair treatment (man 2) and relief (man 3). However, initially it is sufficient to help clients understand that people react to the same objective event (loss of job) in different ways because of the different meanings they attach to this event. In classical REBT, meaning is usually considered to be a fusion of 'critical A' and 'B' factors.

storytelling or, to put it another way, how long to let it go on for. We would suggest these guidelines for intervention:

1 Ask for permission to interrupt before the storytelling starts, so the client will be less surprised or affronted when you do.
2 Interrupt if the client begins to repeat himself, for example, 'You've already mentioned that. Have you now given me the gist of the problem?'
3 Interrupt to clarify points in the story, for example, 'What did he actually say that you made yourself so angry about?'
4 Interrupt if the client is going off in all directions and you need to bring him back to the central narrative or establish one, for example, 'There seem to be so many strands to this story. Which one appears to be the most important to you or the one you want to focus on?'
5 Interrupt if the client is long-winded and/or you are struggling to understand his problem, for example, 'Could you sum up for me in a sentence what exactly is the problem you want to work on?'

Your goal is to move your clients away from unstructured storytelling to structured storytelling through the use of the 'ABC' model (Neenan and Dryden, 2001).

## Making 'ABC' sense of the client's story

In the following dialogue, the therapist puts the client's story into an 'ABC' framework:

*Client*: Well, it's all to do with my best friend and what he did. You know we've been friends for a long time. We were in the army together. We watched each other's backs when we were serving in Northern Ireland and I thought it would be the same in Civvy Street. So you think you know a bloke, know what I mean? Then he goes and does something like that and it was unbelievable. I never imagined in a million years he'd do that. It's unbelievable. My best friend and everything and he goes and does that and …

*Therapist:* Can I interrupt you there? I don't understand what the issue is. What was it that your best friend did that you found 'unbelievable'?

*[The therapist is attempting to focus the client's mind on the substance of the problem – clarifying the 'A' – thereby stopping him from talking in general terms about it.]*

*Client:* He pulled out of a business deal we'd set up. I thought we were going into business together and he pulls the plug at the last minute. I thought I could trust him totally. I was gobsmacked and …

*Therapist:* When you say 'gobsmacked', are you referring to how you felt about what he did?

*[The therapist is now focused on eliciting 'C'.]*

*Client:* Yeah. I was livid, I felt totally let down.

*Therapist:* When you say 'livid, let down' does that refer to anger and hurt?

*Client:* Yeah, angry and hurt, it's all swirling round in my mind, but I really feel anguish over what he did to me.

*Therapist:* So is anguish the best word to describe how you feel?

*[The therapist uses the client's term for 'C' rather than shoehorn him into using 'REBT approved' terms for disturbed emotional Cs.]*

*Client:* Yeah. That really seems to sum it up for me.

*Therapist:* What are you most anguished about in regard to him pulling out of the deal?

*[The therapist is attempting to find the client's 'critical A'.]*

*Client:* There are so many things: our friendship is gone, I feel now that I didn't really know him after all, I wonder why I didn't see it coming, can I ever trust my judgement again, he destroyed my dream of having my own business, I don't feel I can really trust anyone again … I don't know.

*Therapist:* Can you pick one of those issues so we can focus on it?

*[The therapist does not want to examine each item in the client's list to determine which one is the most relevant to his anguish. This might produce more 'anguish' for the client with the number of questions he would*

*be asked and a lot of headscratching for the therapist trying to make sense of the replies in her search for the often elusive 'critical A'.]*

Client:       [*ponders*] That he destroyed my dream of having my own business.

Therapist:  Is that the worst aspect of it for you?

Client:       I think it's that he betrayed me. I think that's what hurts the most. I'll never forgive him for that.

*[The client refers again to hurt, which seems to be synonymous with what he calls anguish. The theme in hurt is betrayal.]*

Therapist:  Okay, let's write down what we've uncovered so far.

At this point the client is a little unsure if his friend's betrayal is 'what hurts the most' but it can be considered as a reasonable or a near-'critical A' that merits clinical examination. The therapist avoids what can be a trap for some REBT therapists: an almost obsessional search for *the* 'critical A' that exhausts both client and therapist.

Situation = My best friend pulled out of a business deal with me

Critical A = He betrayed me

B = ?

C = Anguish

The therapist now explains to the client the role of rigid 'musts' and 'shoulds' and their extreme derivatives in largely determining emotional disturbance. The client only acknowledges the 'should' in his thinking ('That should is rock-solid. There's no way on this earth that he should have pulled out of that deal'); he is not convinced by other aspects of REBT's view of disturbance-inducing thinking and the therapist has no desire to engage in time-wasting arguments over the 'correctness' of the REBT viewpoint.

Therapist:  So the 'B', or irrational belief, is: 'He shouldn't have betrayed me. I'll never forgive him for that.' Does that belief help to explain your anguish at 'C'?

# Accepting emotional responsibility

Little, if any, therapeutic benefit will be achieved if your client stead-fastly points his finger at the 'situation' or at 'A' as the source of his emotional problems; so take time to help your client turn his attention away from 'A' to focus on 'B'. To resume the dialogue:

*Client*:     Of course not. My best friend made me feel this way. I don't see the belief as irrational at all. It's common sense.

*[The client does not accept emotional responsibility.]*

*Therapist*:     So if your best friend is responsible for causing you this anguish, does that mean he is also responsible for reduc-ing it or making it go away? Is that common sense too?

*Client*:     I don't know. We haven't spoken to each other since he pulled out of the deal. I'm certainly not going to go out of my way to talk to him, let alone ask him for help.

*Therapist*:     So will you be stuck in a state of limbo until he calls you and tries to make amends? That's supposing he is going to do that. Will it make any difference anyway because you said you are not going to forgive him?

*Client*:     That's true, I'm not going to forgive him. I don't want to rely on him for anything, ever again.

*Therapist*:     But, despite having said that, it seems to me that the logic of your argument is that he is the only person who can make you feel better. Apparently, you are unable to help yourself.

*Client*:     Okay, I'm getting the point: I need to do something to help myself. What is it then?

*Therapist*:     By taking control of how you emotionally respond to this situation. Your anguish belongs to you, no one else gave it to you. That's the bad news. The good news is that it is within your control to reduce it, irrespective of what your best friend does or does not do, by examining and chang-ing that belief of yours.

*Client*:     Okay. I suppose I could give it a try, but I still don't like that word 'irrational'.

*[The client is warming to the idea of emotional responsibility.]*

| | |
|---|---|
| *Therapist*: | What would you like to call it? |
| *Client*: | Well, it's keeping me stuck, isn't it? |
| *Therapist*: | Shall we call it 'the SB: stuck belief'? |
| *Client*: | Yeah. I'll go along with that. [*ponders*] You know all this talk about my anguish makes me seem pathetic, doesn't it? |

The client's last comment in the dialogue above may indicate the presence of a meta-emotional problem. See the later section in this chapter.

# Establishing goals

Ensure that your client's goals are within his control otherwise he will be looking to others to provide the solution for his emotional problems (as the client was doing in the above dialogue). In order to determine if your client has achieved his goals, measure change along the following three major dimensions:

1 **Frequency**: does your client make himself disturbed less frequently than before?
2 **Intensity**: when your client makes himself disturbed, does he do so with less intensity than before?
3 **Duration**: when your client makes himself disturbed, does he do so for shorter periods of time than before?

Encourage your client to keep a record of his disturbed feelings using these three dimensions so that he can plot his progress. To return to the dialogue:

| | |
|---|---|
| *Therapist*: | Now, if your goal is to be less anguished, how does your present level of anguish display itself? |
| *Client*: | Well, I brood a lot in the evenings when I come home from work. My wife tells me to snap out of it. |
| *Therapist*: | How long do you brood for in the evenings? |

| Client: | I don't know – a couple of hours perhaps. |
|---|---|
| Therapist: | So if you were feeling less anguished, how would that affect the time you spend brooding? |
| Client: | It'd be much less. |
| Therapist: | And what would you be doing with the time instead? |

Here the therapist is encouraging the client to put the goal in positive terms (what he wants to do or have more of) rather than stating it in negative terms (what he wants less of). 'Stating goals positively represents a self-affirming position' (Cormier and Cormier, 1985: 223). The client responds:

| Client: | I'd be spending it with my wife and kids and I'd be in a better mood. Also, I'd be pottering about in the garden on these warm, summer evenings. I like doing that sort of thing. |
|---|---|
| Therapist: | So those will be some of the ways that we can see that positive change is occurring. Right? [*Client nods.*] |

## Meta-emotional problems

As we showed in Chapter 1 (see p. 7), meta-emotion means disturbing ourselves about our primary emotional problems, for example, guilt about feeling angry, ashamed of feeling anxious. It is important to be on the alert for the possible presence of meta-emotional problems as they can impede your client's progress. If a meta-emotional problem is detected, then discuss with your client if this emotion should now become the focus of your clinical attention, as shown in the following dialogue:

| Therapist: | You said earlier that 'all this talk about my anguish makes me seem pathetic'. Do you see yourself as pathetic for experiencing this anguish? |
|---|---|
| Client: | Sometimes. |
| Therapist: | How do you feel when, on these occasions, you see yourself as pathetic? |

*Client*:      I suppose I feel ashamed of myself for not 'snapping out of it' as my wife says I should do. It's being weak, isn't it?

*Therapist*:      I wouldn't agree with that but we can discuss that idea later. For now, I would like to find out if you feel ashamed of yourself at this moment for not 'snapping out of it'?

*[The therapist does not want to get sidetracked into discussing the client's meta-emotional problem unless it will block him from working on his primary emotional problem.]*

*Client*:      No, not really.

*Therapist*:      So will this shame prevent you from focusing on your anguish and how to tackle it?

*Client*:      Shouldn't think so. How can I be sure though?

*Therapist*:      If you spend more time absorbed by your shame than you do listening to me! If your mind appears to be elsewhere, I will point this out to you.

*Client*:      Okay, seems reasonable.

*Therapist*:      So shall we turn our attention now to examining this stuck belief of yours, 'He shouldn't have betrayed me. I'll never forgive him for that'?

*Client*:      Okay, but I'm not convinced yet it's the main cause of my anguish. I'll keep an open mind on it though.

*Therapist*:      That'll do.

We see that the client is still expressing his doubts about the concept of emotional responsibility. The therapist does not expect her client, or any client, to be a strong believer in this concept in the early stage of therapy. It is enough that the client will keep an 'open mind' on the subject.

## Chapter summary

In this chapter we have seen how the therapist has helped the client to pinpoint what he considers is the crucial aspect of his presenting problem. He has idiosyncratically defined his disturbance-inducing beliefs and disturbed feelings, and is prepared to be receptive to the concept of emotional responsibility. The next step is to dispute or examine his 'stuck beliefs'.

# FOUR

## Disputing

DiGiuseppe states that 'disputing irrational beliefs has always been at
the heart of RE[B]T' (1991: 173) and is the principal activity of experienced REBT therapists. The *Concise Oxford English Dictionary* provides a definition of disputing as 'question the truth or correctness
or validity of (a statement, alleged fact, etc.)'. Disputing in REBT is a
questioning or examining of your clients' irrational beliefs (these
beliefs can be REBT 'approved' or idiosyncratically defined) in order to
lead to the development of flexible and non-extreme belief systems.[1]
Disputing is not about arguing, being abrasive or rude, in-your-face
confrontation or engaging in power struggles; if some of these things
do occur, then pay attention to your beliefs that may be driving such
behaviour, for example, 'I have to prove my competence as a therapist
by getting the client to accept my arguments.'

Disputing helps clients to see that their beliefs

> are both *theoretically untenable* (e.g., are unfactual or tautological,
> contain internal inconsistencies, are based on false premises, are
> non-sequiturial) and are *impractical* or *impossible* (e.g., lead to poor
> results, cannot be obtained or accomplished, result in short range gain
> at the expense of long range cost). (Grieger and Boyd, 1980: 130; original
> italics)

---

[1] Clients frequently cling to their irrational beliefs with considerable tenacity. Ellis (1979b)
has advised therapists to attack such beliefs with force and energy. While a vigorous
disputing approach may work with some clients, others may see it as intimidating or
overwhelming; therefore, do not be a one-note disputer. In our experience, the quiet
presentation of telling arguments can work wonders in eroding a client's support for
her irrational beliefs.

This outcome is achieved by encouraging your clients to reflect on what they believe – an activity that may for some clients be painful, unsettling or effortful. As Blackburn observes:

> Human beings are relentlessly capable of reflecting on themselves. We might do something out of habit, but then we can begin to reflect on the habit. We can habitually think things, and then reflect on what we are thinking. We can ask ourselves (or sometimes we get asked by other people) whether we know what we are talking about. To answer that we need to reflect on our own positions, our own understanding of what we are saying, our own sources of authority. (2001: 4)

Helping clients to reflect on and challenge aspects of their thinking, empirically testing their beliefs and developing alternative, more self-helping ways of viewing themselves, others and the world results in them 'functioning at a much fuller realization of their thought potential' (Grieger and Boyd, 1980: 131).

## Belief levels

Irrational beliefs can be 'stated at varying levels of abstraction' (DiGiuseppe, 1991: 186). The level of abstraction ranges from beliefs held in specific situations (for example, 'I must have my partner's approval'), across general situations (for example, 'I must have the approval of my friends and colleagues') and globally (for example, 'Everyone must approve of me'). An irrational belief that is challenged at a general level (demanding approval from friends and colleagues) will tackle a greater number of activating events that the client disturbs herself about than an irrational belief held in a specific situation (demanding the approval of her partner). Similarly, the more abstract the rational belief, the more generalizable and disturbance-reducing it will be.

A common mistake made by some REBTers, particularly trainees, is to presume that a client holds a general version of a situation-specific irrational belief and then start disputing it thereby leaving the client feeling baffled by the therapist's behaviour. For example, a client says that it is unfair he did not get promoted after years of loyal service to the company and that his company should have treated him better; the therapist asks: 'Why must the world treat you fairly?' The client, perplexed by the therapist's question, replies: 'It's the company's behaviour I'm unhappy with, not how the world treats me.' Disputing should start with a situation-specific irrational belief and only move to more general or core irrational beliefs if the client acknowledges their existence and wants to work on them.[2]

## Formulaic disputing

This means disputing in an unintelligent or slavish way. In many REBT textbooks, including our own, a formula for disputing is offered to therapists. Such a formula is asking the client if her belief is rigid or flexible, extreme or non-extreme, and questioning the logical, empirical and pragmatic status of the belief (Neenan and Dryden, 2000). Providing a formula is only meant to be a guide to disputing: it is not intended to provide therapists with a complete 'disputing kit'. Formulaic disputing, which we hear a lot of, often goes something like this:

*Trainee*: Is your belief 'I must never show any weaknesses' rigid or flexible?

*Client*: I suppose it does sound somewhat rigid.

*Trainee*: That's right. Do you think that calling yourself 'weak' for showing a weakness is an extreme way of judging yourself for being a fallible human being?

---

[2] As DiGiuseppe (1991) notes, a situation-specific belief resembles a self-statement more than an unspoken philosophy. Making manifest and disputing an unspoken irrational philosophy leads to a more elegant outcome for the client as a wide number of adverse or potentially adverse situations are covered by her new rational outlook which a situation-specific self-statement would obviously not be able to encompass.

| | |
|---|---|
| *Client*: | I suppose it is a bit over the top. |
| *Trainee*: | Right. Now does it logically follow that because you strongly prefer not to show any weaknesses therefore you must not show them? |
| *Client*: | Well, if you put it like that, I suppose it doesn't logically follow. |
| *Trainee*: | It doesn't, does it? Now, is it true that you have never shown a weakness? |
| *Client*: | I suppose it's not true. I don't really know. |
| *Trainee*: | Not true then. Now, where is it going to get you holding onto that belief, 'I must never show any weaknesses because, if I do, this will prove to others I'm weak'? |
| *Client*: | I suppose it will give me some trouble now and again. |
| *Trainee*: | Probably a lot of trouble. Can you now see why your belief is irrational? |
| *Client*: | Hmm. |

The outcome of such disputing is usually highly unsatisfactory for both therapist and client: the former believes that disputing cannot be as straightforward as this while the latter remains unconvinced by the points the therapist is making, as indicated by her 'I suppose …' replies. Disputing as if you are on automatic pilot is unlikely to engage your clients in a productive discussion of their irrational beliefs, let alone lead to constructive changes in them.

## Creative disputing

This means moving beyond textbook formulas for disputing and *thinking for yourself*. What arguments can you devise that will help to turn the tide in your clients' irrational thinking? In a chapter called 'The Best Rational Arguments', Paul Hauck comments that:

> Your strength as an RE[B]T counselor is measured in part by the ease with which you can call up rational arguments to counterattack irrational arguments. But, in addition to ease, you also seek arguments that have uniqueness, humor, and an overriding impression of correctness. The more such arguments you possess, the better counselor you will be. (1980: 117)

While we are not denigrating the use of standard arguments (for example, 'Where's the evidence?'), we would urge you to be looking for what Hauck calls 'fresh debate material'. Using the same arguments with all of your clients is bound to lead to staleness and boredom in therapy (for some fresh debate material see Neenan and Dryden, 2002). To return to the above dialogue, it is important for the trainee to try out some of his own ideas and monitor the client's reaction to them in order to determine which ones capture her attention:

| | |
|---|---|
| *Trainee*: | Now your belief is 'I must not show any weaknesses'. Right? [*client nods*] Do you see coming to therapy as a sign of weakness? |
| *Client*: | Er … I don't know. |
| *Trainee*: | Do you see it as a sign of strength? |
| *Client*: | I don't suppose it's that. People come to therapy because they can't sort out their own problems. I suppose coming to therapy is a sign of weakness. |
| *Trainee*: | So how does that support your belief that you *must* not show any weaknesses? In other words, is your belief true? |
| *Client*: | [*shrugs her shoulders*] Well, I suppose it isn't true after all. |

[*The client seems uninterested in her own conclusion. The trainee tries another argument.*]

| | |
|---|---|
| *Trainee*: | When you say that you must not show any weaknesses, does that mean you do have some weaknesses but others must not see them? |
| *Client*: | [*concentrating*] I do have some weaknesses like feeling anxious when I meet new people or being the centre of attention. I try to keep myself under control because I don't want them to think badly of me. |

[*The client is becoming engaged in the conversation.*]

| | |
|---|---|
| *Trainee*: | You say you try to keep yourself under control so they won't think badly of you, but how do you know your attempts at control are successful? |

*Client*: What do you mean?

*Trainee*: Well, does that 'must' statement guarantee that your weaknesses will not be exposed to other people and therefore you will avoid being judged negatively by them?

*Client*: I know it won't guarantee it and I'm sure other people do see how nervous I am, no matter what I say to myself. The funny thing is the more I try to suppress my nervousness, the more nervous I become. I don't really get much peace of mind.

*Trainee*: Would you like to start giving yourself some peace of mind by changing that belief of yours?

*Client*: How do I do that?

*Trainee*: First, release the pressure in your mind by giving up that 'must'. Second, learn to accept yourself with your weaknesses irrespective of how others see you. And, third, learn to tackle constructively those behaviours you call 'weaknesses'.

*Client*: That's a tall order.

*Trainee*: Maybe, but your way hasn't worked so far, so are you willing to give my way a try? You can always go back to your ways if you don't like mine or they don't work out.

Pointing out to clients that they can return to their old ways of thinking, feeling and behaving shows them that you are not trying to 'force' a new way on them and they remain in control of the change process.

*Client*: [*nodding her head*] Okay. I'm willing to give your way a try.

*Trainee*: If you find my way helpful, I hope you will take it over and make it your way.

Initial disputing has not dislodged the client's irrational belief nor was it intended to, but it has presented her with the possibility of developing a different perspective on tackling her problems – clients do not usually give up their irrational ideas unless they have alternative ideas to replace them with. Disputing is usually carried out in each session to ameliorate the client's original problem, tackle new ones that emerge, overcome resistance and remove obstacles to change (self-disputation is also required when some of your beliefs become obstacles to client change, for example, 'The client has to accept my arguments because they are right and hers are wrong').

# From formulaic to creative disputing

Earlier in this chapter we cautioned you against the use of formulaic disputing and encouraged you to be creative in disputing your clients' irrational beliefs. However, we realize that you are unlikely to be creative at the outset of your therapy career. REBT, in this respect, is like jazz: improvisation is the essence of jazz but can only be achieved once the player has mastered the basics of his instrument. To improvise without learning the basics first will lead to a cacophony of sound. Similarly in REBT, attempting creative disputing without learning the basics first will lead to a discordant 'sound' of ill-considered arguments, conflicting ideas, feel-good phrasemaking and rambling reflections.

To avoid this outcome, it is important to understand that at the beginning of your career you may sound formulaic in your use of disputing strategies, but once you have mastered the basics you can go on to improvise and be creative – the 'boring' part before the exciting part. What we strongly discourage you from doing is resting on your laurels once you have learnt the basics of disputing. The REBT therapists who do this are the ones who sound formulaic in their disputing work and are also the ones who are the least effective disputers.

# Preparing your clients for disputing

Disputing can be an uncomfortable experience for clients as they are being asked, in essence, to defend their beliefs. In order to pave the way for disputing and avoid the impression that you are attacking your clients, there are a number of activities to carry out:

1   Review the 'ABCs' of the client's presenting problem.
2   Remind the client of the importance of the 'B'–'C' connection, that is, that irrational beliefs (B) largely determine emotional consequences (C). This will help her to see the sense in disputing 'B' rather than attempting to change the 'situation' or the adverse aspect of the situation at 'A'.
3   Help the client to understand that her new 'C' (emotional goal) is achieved by changing 'B': emotional change flows from belief change.
4   Explain to your client what is involved in the disputing process (that is, an examination of her irrational beliefs) and what is not involved (for example, arguing, 'brainwashing').

# Mixing basic and creative disputing

Elements of basic and creative disputing are likely to be found, or rather heard, in the session audiotapes of experienced REBT practitioners. Such a mixture is present in the main therapist–client dialogue of this book, to which we now return.

> *Therapist:*   Just to recap on what we've done so far: you're feeling anguished about your best friend pulling out of a business deal with you. Your belief about this situation, which we've agreed to call the 'stuck belief', is 'He shouldn't have betrayed me. I'll never forgive him for that' [*client nods*]. Now I know you're not convinced but you are prepared to consider the possibility that your belief about your best friend's behaviour rather than the behaviour itself is largely responsible for your current anguish [*client nods*]. If you want to reduce your anguish and get yourself into a better mood, then you need to get yourself unstuck from that belief. To do that, we will carefully examine that belief and decide if there are more helpful ways of thinking about

|          | your problem. I'll be offering you arguments to consider, but I certainly won't be trying to force you to accept my viewpoint. Okay? |
|----------|-----|
| *Client*: | That's okay with me. How do we begin then? |
| *Therapist*: | Now you said previously that your 'should' was 'rock solid'. |
| *Client*: | That's right. |
| *Therapist*: | Does that rock solid 'should' allow you to accept the reality of what actually occurred, integrate that painful episode into your experience and move on with your life? |

[*The therapist is seeking to discover if the client sees his irrational belief as realistic, adaptable and conducive to therapeutic movement in his life.*]

| *Client*: | Of course not! How can I 'move on', as you say, when he betrayed me? |
|----------|-----|
| *Therapist*: | I'll come to the issue of betrayal a little later if I may, but as long as your 'should' remains rock solid, what will happen to your anguish? |

[*The therapist is disconnecting the rock-solid 'should' from the issue of betrayal. Separate consideration of these areas may help the client to be more objective in his discussion of them.*]

| *Client*: | Nothing will happen to it, it'll just still be there. |
|----------|-----|
| *Therapist*: | And how will that help you to reduce your anguish then? |
| *Client*: | It won't. Do you expect me to forget all about it then? |
| *Therapist*: | I don't expect you to forget it, but it's the way you hang onto what's happened that's keeping your anguish going rather than diminishing it. Your rock-solid 'should' is, in essence, a demand that your best friend should not have acted in the way that he did at that time. |

[*In other words, the empirical reality at that time should have been other than it was. The therapist is pointing out the absurdity of the client's reality-denying 'should'.*]

| *Client*: | Are you taking his side then? |
|----------|-----|
| *Therapist*: | I'm not taking his side. I'm trying to encourage you to step back from the problem and try to view it more objectively. |

Look, who ultimately determines what your best friend does – you or him?

[*If rock-solid 'shoulds' were realistic, then they would determine his best friend's behaviour irrespective of what the best friend wanted to do.*]

Client:     Well, he does obviously. Am I supposed to feel sorry for him or something?

Therapist:  I'm not asking you to feel sorry for him. People act in the ways that they do based upon what's happening in their life at any given moment. Therefore, what's important to him will not always coincide with what you see as important in your life.

[*The therapist is pointing out the unpalatable truth that the client is not necessarily at the centre of his best friend's universe; other factors or priorities compete for attention in his best friend's life.*]

Client:     But he said he was going to go into business with me. He gave me his word.

Therapist:  And I'm sure he meant it at the time but circumstances change and people cannot always keep to what they've agreed or promised. Have you ever broken a promise?

[*The therapist does a little 'mind-reading' regarding the client's best friend in order to emphasize the point that what is promised is not necessarily translated into later action, for whatever reason.*]

Client:     Yes, but it wasn't a really important promise like going into business with someone.

Therapist:  Who determines the importance of the broken promise: you or the person on the receiving end of your broken promise?

Client:     [*sheepishly*] I suppose they do.

Therapist:  Okay. Let's get back to that immovable 'should' in your mind [*tapping head*]. Such 'shoulds' are reality-denying: reality should have been other than it was at that time; in other words, the business deal had gone through because your best friend had kept his word.

[*The therapist returns to the issue of what was and compares it with the client's dictates of how things should have been. The therapist is trying to encourage the client to see the futility of clinging to his 'immovable should'.*]

Client:      Well, he should have done.

Therapist:   If you hang on to that 'should', do you think it will act as a time machine and take you back in time to alter reality in your favour?

[*The therapist is imagining the client as a time traveller who can return to the past and rewrite it. In reality, is the past irrevocable or a tabula rasa?*]

Client:      I know that's impossible, there is no time machine. It sounds silly when you put it like that. What's happened has happened. You just have to get on with your life. [*ponders*] You know when I was serving in Northern Ireland I had good friends who were killed, wounded, maimed for life. You had to focus on the job, that's what kept you going. If you dwelt on all that unpleasant stuff that was going on, you would lose it up here [*tapping the side of his head*] as some blokes did. Then you would be a danger to your comrades. They might not be able to rely on you when things got sticky.

Therapist:   Do you think you now have a job to get on with?

[*The therapist links the client's experiences in Northern Ireland to his present problems in order to encourage the emergence of a problem-solving outlook.*]

Client:      [*nodding*] Deep down I know it's the only thing to do. I've got to move beyond it as my wife says, but not all in one go.

Therapist:   What would you need to tell yourself in order to start moving yourself out of this stuck zone?

[*The therapist focuses the client's attention on how problem-solving is actually going to start.*]

Client:      [*ponders*] Hmm. Well, something like 'It happened, now move forward'.

Therapist:   What would that actually mean? For example, would it mean that you have accepted, without liking it in any way, that your best friend pulled out of the deal?

[*The therapist seeks clarity regarding the meaning of the client's statement.*]

*Client*:       Yes, it would mean that. I've dealt with many difficult situa-
                tions in my life, particularly in the army, and I don't want to
                be defeated by this one.

*Therapist*:    Good. Now, can we turn our attention to the issue of
                betrayal. What do you mean by betrayal?

[*The client may have an idiosyncratic definition of betrayal rather than a
standard dictionary one.*]

*Client*:       Well, that you've been stabbed in the back. You put your
                trust in someone who turns out to be a snake in the grass.

*Therapist*:    Do you think he deliberately set out to deceive you, know-
                ing full well that he was going to pull out of the deal at the
                last minute?

[*The therapist is now encouraging the client to 'mind-read' in order to get
him to consider the totality of his lifelong relationship with his best friend.
Based on the evidence, is his best friend likely to behave in that way?*]

*Client*:       [*shaking his head*] If I'm to be honest, I don't think he would
                do that. I've known him all my life. He pulled me out of a
                few tough scrapes in the army. I shouldn't have called him
                a snake in the grass but when you've put all your trust in
                someone so close …

*Therapist*:    Because you've put all your trust in someone so close to
                you does that person have to meet that trust no matter
                what is happening in their life at any given moment?

[*The 'have to' may be a binding commitment in the client's mind but his
friend may and did have a different view on it.*]

*Client*:       Well, you would expect them to do their best to fulfil it. I would
                try to do my best if somebody put their full trust in me.

*Therapist*:    I'm not talking about 'expect them to' or 'try to', which is per-
                fectly reasonable, but a rock-solid 'have to', no matter what.

[*The therapist is emphasizing the distinction between flexible expectations
and rigid, uncompromising demands.*]

*Client*:       You mean like my rock-solid 'should' [*therapist nods*]. Well, I
                suppose their life cannot revolve around that rock-solid

'have to'. I don't live their life, so I may not know what's really going on. Circumstances change in their life which I'm not aware of.

Therapist: That's right. Nothing stays constant. No matter what any-one promises you, you cannot guarantee that those prom-ises will be carried out. That's the grim reality. So we come back to whether or not you will accept, albeit reluctantly, this grim reality or continue to hang onto that rock-solid 'should' – 'He shouldn't have betrayed me.'

[*The therapist sums up the choices for the client: continue to deny reality or reluctantly accept it – stasis or change.*]

Client: No, I don't want to hang onto it and you've given me some ideas about betrayal which never occurred to me. I expect you want me to forgive him now.

Therapist: That's entirely up to you. Reducing your anguish over this matter is the main goal. You don't need to forgive him in order to reduce your anguish. The two issues are not related.

[*Forgiveness is optional; the important point is for the client to make peace with himself over past events and move on. Making peace with himself can be facilitated by absorbing some of the realistic points made in therapy.*]

Client: There's a lot for me to think about. How do I get my head around all this?

Therapist: As the session is drawing to a close, now would be a good time to answer that in terms of your homework.

## Chapter summary

In this chapter we have seen the client being introduced to disputing. The therapist has presented the client with some ideas for him to consider which may have the effect of 'chipping away' at his irrational beliefs. Therapist-initiated disputing is expected to lead to self-disputing as part of the client's developing role as his own therapist.

# FIVE

## Homework

### Rationale for homework
### tasks

Homework has been an important feature of REBT since its inception in 1955 (Wessler and Wessler, 1980). If your client sees you for one hour every week, what is he or she going to do with the other 111 hours before the next appointment (we assume that the client has eight hours sleep per night)? As Persons remarks:

> Situations that arouse powerful affect probably involve the patient's key underlying ideas, and the ability to work on these when they are activated offers a potent opportunity for change that would be missed if all therapeutic work took place during therapy sessions. (1989: 141–2)

Homework is the activity carried out by clients between sessions and puts into practice the learning that has occurred within your office.[1] Clients can claim that their irrational thinking is changing, but how is this claim to be verified if they do not provide behavioural evidence of such change? For example, a client who states that he can now stand doing boring tasks still procrastinates over doing them. Has he really

---

[1] For some clients the word homework 'often has surplus meaning, bringing to mind teacher–student relationships, with the client seeing himself or herself in a subservient role rather than as a joint partner in a collaborative venture' (Meichenbaum, 1985: 44). To uncover surplus meaning, ask your clients if they experience any negative reactions when you talk of homework. If they do experience such reactions, then use other terms such as real-life activities or self-help assignments.

tackled his discomfort intolerance ideas about such tasks? We doubt it. We might say that he has cognition without ignition (that is, cognitive change without accompanying behavioural change). Unless a nascent rational philosophy is acted upon, it will not be internalized and the client will be marooned at the level of intellectual insight into his problems; therefore, homework is a vital part of REBT practice, never an optional extra on the therapeutic agenda.

Homework tasks allow clients to develop competence and confidence in facing their problems and, therefore, they are less likely to become dependent on you as the agent of change in their lives; in other words, they are becoming their own self-therapist. For clients who drag their feet over carrying out homework, point out to them 'that compliance with self-help assignments may be the most important predictor of therapeutic success' (Burns, 1989: 545). With those clients who are consistently recalcitrant in executing their homework assignments, a contract can be used whereby further therapy is contingent upon clients completing their homework tasks. Non-compliance in carrying out their homework tasks means these clients are likely to maintain the status quo in their life, that is, remain emotionally disturbed.[2]

# Types of homework assignments

These can be described as cognitive, behavioural, emotive and imaginal.

## Cognitive tasks

These 'rely solely on verbal interchange between therapist and client (within sessions), between the client and himself (written or thinking homework), and between author and client (reading and listening to

---

[2] In the final analysis, if one of your clients steadfastly refuses to carry out homework assignments, you will have to decide whether to continue to see him for REBT and hope that he might do some homework eventually or refer him to a different type of therapy where homework is not an integral therapeutic feature.

tapes as homework' (Wessler and Wessler, 1980: 113). These tasks help clients to become more informed about the theory and practice of REBT and thereby deepen their intellectual insight into their problems and what steps are needed to overcome them.

## Reading

Reading REBT materials to promote therapeutic change is called bibliotherapy. There is a substantial body of REBT self-help literature, for example, *Hold Your Head Up High* by Paul Hauck (1991) and *10 Steps to Positive Living* by Windy Dryden (1994). Reading self-help literature in the absence of therapy does not usually lead to lasting change as people infrequently act in a persistent and forceful way to implement the ideas contained in this literature; or, as one of us (WD) has written, self-help books do not work in the sense that reading them does not in itself promote psychotherapeutic change (Dryden, 1998b).

You should, ideally, have read the literature you recommend to your clients so you can discuss it with some authority when the client refers to it and correct any misconceptions the client may have developed about what she has read (for example, 'It seems to me that enlightened self-interest is just a clever way of saying "I'm going to a be selfish"'). Always ascertain if your client has any reading difficulties as she may be reluctant or embarrassed to tell you.

## Listening

This can be to CDs of lectures by leading REBTers, for example, Albert Ellis on *Unconditionally Accepting Yourself and Others* (1986) and Ray DiGiuseppe discussing *What Do I Do With My Anger: Hold It In or Let It Out?* (1989) or to relaxation CDs as an adjunct to a cognitive restructuring of clients' anxiogenic thinking.

REBT favours clients recording their therapy sessions in order to listen to them away from your office. Listening to the recordings between sessions often brings greater understanding of important points made in the session – points missed or inadequately processed at the time by the client because he was, for example, overly disturbed or reluctant to admit he did not understand what you were saying.[3] On their own, clients are likely to feel less inhibited or distracted and thereby more able to focus on the session content and bring their comments about it to the next session.

## Writing

A formal method of challenging irrational beliefs is by encouraging clients to guide themselves through the ABCDE model of emotional disturbance and change by asking a series of questions which they can write down. An example of a self-help form is:

| | | |
|---|---|---|
| Situation | = | Describe clearly and concisely. |
| Critical A | = | What am I most disturbed about in this situation? |
| Beliefs | = | What is my irrational belief about this situation? |
| Consequences | = | What are my disturbed emotions, behaviours and subsequent thinking in this situation? |
| Disputing | = | What is a different way to think about this situation through disputing my irrational beliefs? |
| Effects | = | What are my new beliefs, emotions, behaviours and subsequent thinking in this situation? |

This example of cognitive homework is given to clients only after they have gained proficiency in the use of such self-help forms through in-session practice.

Other tasks include writing essays that explore rational ideas, for example, a client who believes that she must always perform perfectly agrees to write a composition entitled 'Why fallibility (imperfection) is an ineradicable part of human nature'. Clients can also keep diaries to

---

[3] Some clients may become disturbed when listening to the session tapes (for example, 'I sound so pathetic with all the whining I keep on doing'; 'I can't believe I talk so much nonsense'). These reactions can be processed at the next session and a more balanced appraisal sought (for example, 'My whining is a product of not knowing what to do about my problem. This state of affairs will now hopefully change with the help of my therapist'). If some clients insist that the taping must stop because they do not like listening to themselves, then comply with this request.

record their upsetting thoughts and disturbed feelings and the situations in which they occur. Keeping a diary helps clients to note constructive changes in these thoughts and feelings.

## Behavioural tasks

You behave as you think. Forcefully and persistently acting against one's self-defeating ideas not only undermines these ideas but also strengthens new ways of thinking and feeling. Therefore, behavioural tasks serve as a means to achieve a cognitive end (that is, philosophical change):

> For example, if clients believe they cannot stand waiting for events, they are asked to practice postponing gratifications. If they believe that they cannot stand rejection, they are encouraged to seek it out. If they believe that they need something, they are exhorted to do without. If they believe their worth is based on doing well, they are asked to purposely do poorly. (Walen et al., 1992: 169)

Two of the most frequently used homework tasks are stay-in-there exercises and risk-taking activities (Grieger and Boyd, 1980). Stay-in-there exercises encourage clients to enter the most aversive situation straightaway (for example, getting into a lift and going all the way to the top floor) or working through a hierarchy of aversive situations, from least to most aversive (for example, one or two floors at a time; going all the way to the top floor may be several weeks away or longer). Risk-taking activities involve clients undertaking tasks they may fail at or not do well or may incur criticism, disapproval or rejection from others (for example, speaking up in a group to voice one's opinions instead of always agreeing with the majority view in order not to be the odd one out).

It is important that in both types of behavioural assignments you encourage your clients to repeat their rational beliefs at the same time as they carry out these assignments. While thinking rationally is the primary means of achieving emotional insight (rational beliefs deeply and consistently held), behavioural tasks are very important because clients may doubt the efficacy of their new rational beliefs if they are not acted upon.

## Emotive tasks

These are designed to engage fully clients' disturbed feelings in order to ameliorate them through a sustained and vigorous disputing of ingrained irrational ideas. The most well known emotive technique is shame-attacking exercises (Ellis, 1969).[4] This encourages clients to act in a 'shameful' way in real life in order to attract criticism or provoke disapproval (for example, a man goes into a chemist's shop and asks for the smallest condoms possible) or design an exercise that is more relevant to the client's problem (for example, a client with strong approval needs puts his overheads upside-down when giving a presentation to his colleagues). Simultaneously with this behavioural component of the exercise, clients are reminded to dispute vigorously their shame-inducing beliefs: 'Just because I acted in a foolish manner does not mean I'm foolish'.

Such exercises are designed to teach clients (1) to strive for self-acceptance and refrain from self-denigration; (2) that they frequently overestimate the negative reactions of others to their behaviour; (3) that it is not awful to behave stupidly or reveal a weakness; (4) and that the disapproving looks and comments of others cannot 'crush' or humiliate them. It is important to note that

---

[4] I (WD) have suggested that these exercises could more accurately be called 'embarrassment-attacking exercises because it seems to me that one of the differences between shame and embarrassment is that you are more likely to feel ashamed when you reveal something very inadequate about yourself, whereas embarrassment is less serious' (Dryden, 1991: 38). Gilbert makes a similar point and adds: 'shame-attacking exercises which involve acting in mildly embarrassing ways … are inappropriate in severe depressive-shame' (2000: 166). We might say that whether the person experiences shame or embarrassment depends on how he evaluates himself on the basis of others' responses to his shame-attacking exercise. On balance, most of the tasks clients perform are probably embarrassment-attacking exercises.

shame-attacking exercises should not put clients or others in harm's way, violate their ethical standards, break the law or bring about self-defeating consequences such as losing their job or jeopardizing their promotion chances.

## Imagery tasks

These tasks use mental images or pictures to dispute clients' irrational beliefs. Imagery tasks often involve using rational-emotive imagery (REI; Maultsby and Ellis, 1974). One example of REI is to ask a client to close her eyes and vividly imagine an adverse event where she experiences a disturbed feeling (for example, angry about her husband flirting with a woman at a party). The client is urged to experience the full force of her disturbed feeling and then, without altering any details of the adverse event, to change her feeling to a non-disturbed one or diminish the intensity of the disturbed feeling (for example, irritated about her husband's flirting). The client is asked to open her eyes and report how this emotional shift was achieved. The ideal answer is that this shift occurred when the client replaced her irrational belief (for example, 'He absolutely shouldn't be flirting with that woman') with a rational belief (for example, 'I know he's flirting with her and I don't like it, but I recognize that he does not have to do what I want. However, because I really don't like it, I shall speak to him about his behaviour when we get home').

Obviously it is important to elicit feedback from the client to determine if the imagery exercise was carried out in the prescribed way. The client might reveal that emotional change was achieved by, for example, distraction ('I imagined myself walking into another room so as not to see what he was doing'), making the event more tolerable ('He won't get anywhere with her. She's too posh for him') and engaging in rationalizing rather than rational thinking ('That's the whole point of a party – to let your hair down. That's all he was doing, having a good time').

## Happiness assignments

These are not routinely mentioned in the REBT literature but point out to clients that REBT is 'not merely working to dispel misery, but actively working to *promote happiness*' (Walen et al., 1992: 269; original italics). You can discuss with your clients what things give them pleasure and encourage them to engage in some of these activities alongside the 'unexciting' side of therapy – the work between sessions. Pleasure does not have to be put on hold until clients' emotional problems are resolved.

## Negotiating homework tasks using the criterion of challenging, but not overwhelming

Some clients might take 'tiny steps' in the problem-solving process which convince them they are getting nowhere with their snail-like progress or reinforce their discomfort intolerance ideas about the hard work of change (for example, 'I can't bear this discomfort'). Other clients might 'bite off more than they can chew' and conclude that feeling overwhelmed by the tasks facing them means they have wiped out the progress they have made (for example, 'I've gone back to square one'). A middle way between 'too little, too slow' and 'too much, too fast', is 'challenging, but not overwhelming', that is, tasks that take clients outside of their comfort zone but without losing sight of it. For example, a client who was procrastinating over tackling some tedious paperwork agreed to work on it for 30 minutes each day; attempting to complete it in one sitting would be too effortful for him. Negotiated homework tasks can be graded as IC (insufficiently challenging), CNO (challenging, but not overwhelming) or TC (too challenging) from the standpoint of your client's current skills and progress.

## 'No lose' formula of homework tasks

This reassures clients that no matter what happens with their homework tasks, some *learning* can be extracted from the experience. Do *not* negotiate homework tasks in terms of success or failure, for example, 'It really is important that you do the homework. If you don't do it, what's the point in you being in therapy?' Focus on what learning the client has derived from:

- Successfully completing the homework task
- Undertaking the homework task but only achieving poor results
- Not doing the homework task.

Information gathered from homework reviews helps you and your client to determine what are the spurs or blocks to task completion. If your client does not carry out his agreed homework tasks, the learning to be extracted from this is stark: he will remain emotionally disturbed and contradict his stated goal of ameliorating his disturbed feelings.

## Can your client see the link between the session work, homework task and her goal?

If your client cannot see this link, then she will be less inclined to carry out the task than if she does she it. For example, a client does not see the relevance of deliberately getting into long queues in the supermarket when it is long meetings, not long queues, that she upsets herself about. If the client's goal is to tolerate, in a non-disturbed way, long meetings and even longer-winded colleagues, then she needs to internalize some forceful coping statements such as 'There is no reason why my time cannot be wasted by long meetings or verbosity but I can look for ways to reduce both if possible'.

# Does your client believe he can carry out the homework assignment?

Even though your clients have agreed to carry out the tasks, do they have sufficient skills to carry them out? Self-efficacy theory (Bandura, 1977) predicts that your client is more likely to carry out a homework task if he believes that he can actually do it than if he lacks what Bandura calls an 'efficacy expectation'. Therefore, carry out a skills assessment and determine what, if any, remedial training may be necessary; if the client does have the necessary skills, ascertain if he is confident about using them. In the latter case, the client does have the skills but lacks an efficacy expectation about their use in a particular setting. For example, a client who can see the difference between failing at an activity but not labelling himself a failure because of it, might need an in-session imaginal rehearsal of putting this distinction into practice when taking his driving test before he does so in reality.

# Trying versus doing

'One of the more common waffling responses when a person is asked to do homework is "I'll try" Notice how little personal responsibility this response communicates' (Grieger, 1991: 60). 'Trying' suggests that some effort might be made but lacks the commitment that 'doing' denotes, that is, persistent and forceful action to get the job done. If some clients have been trying to solve a problem outside of therapy, do they want to continue with this unproductive attitude in therapy? Even when clients say they will 'try harder', they often engage in more of the same behaviour that prevents task completion (for example, a client with social anxiety attends more social functions but still does not initiate conversations). You can demonstrate the difference between trying and doing by asking your clients, for example, to try to stand up or try to leave the room – trying lacks the determination of doing. Clients usually grasp this distinction straightaway but do not expect them to put it into immediate effect!

## When, where and how often?

Vague assurances from the client that the task will be done 'sometime in the next week' do not inspire confidence that the task will actually be done – something more interesting may intervene and push the task to the margins of the client's mind. In order to concentrate the client's mind on the task ahead, ask the following questions: When will you carry out the task?; Where will you do it?; and How often will you do it? Specificity, not vagueness, should guide homework negotiation and thereby make it more likely that the client will execute her agreed assignment.

## Troubleshooting obstacles to homework completion

This involves looking at any actual or potential blocks to homework completion. Once blocks are identified, ways of overcoming them are then discussed. For example, a client might say, 'We are having our house decorated at the moment, so it's going to be a very tight squeeze fitting in the imagery exercises.' You might reply that the client could find some time in his lunch break at work. If your clients keep on finding reasons (a polite term for excuses) why they will have trouble executing their assignments, probe for and address underlying issues, for example, the avoidance of discomfort: 'If you want to feel relatively comfortable in these situations, you first have to make yourself uncomfortable by entering and staying in them until your anxiety subsides. Unpleasant but necessary I'm afraid.' You can liken your role as a troubleshooter to being a 'cognitive cop', that is, apprehending and dealing with clients' thoughts and beliefs that hinder their progress (Neenan and Dryden, 2002).

## Avoid rushing homework negotiation

We hope that we have made clear that homework is vital if therapeutic progress is to occur. We might say: no homework, not much hope for change. Therefore, make provision for homework negotiation in your session agenda; allow 10 minutes or more for novice REBT therapists. If a suitable homework task has emerged earlier in the session and the client has agreed to do it, then less time will be needed at the end of the session to discuss it. Always ensure that you give your clients a written copy of the homework task as a reminder of what they have agreed to do; relying on purely verbal agreement can lead to disagreements when the task is reviewed at the next session (for example, the client thought he was supposed to carry out the task twice a week while you believed the agreement was to do it twice daily).

## Negotiating the client's homework task

In the last chapter the client said near the end of the session 'How do I get my head around all this?' (that is, all the issues that surfaced during the session). A homework task now needs to be agreed that flows logically from the work done in the session:

| | |
|---|---|
| *Therapist*: | What would you like to do as your first homework task based on what we've discussed here today? |
| *Client*: | As I said, there's a lot to think about. Listening to a recording of the session would be a help. I can mull over the points you've been making and my own responses to them. |

[*The client has chosen a cognitive homework task.*]

Therapist:    Good. I'll be interested to hear your comments at our next session. When do you think you'll listen to the tape? The reason I ask that is because clients are sometimes very vague about when they will actually do their tasks.

Client:    Fair enough. I'll listen to it tonight after everyone has gone to bed. I might listen to it more than once.

Therapist:    Can you see any obstacles to listening to it tonight?

Client:    None that I can think of.

Therapist:    Okay. Can I suggest that you write down some comments as you listen to the recording.

[*The therapist has suggested this to help the client be active in the listening process rather than passive.*]

Client:    Yes, that sounds like a good idea.

# Reviewing homework assignments

At the beginning of every session, review your client's homework unless a crisis supervenes that needs to be dealt with immediately and normal agenda setting is suspended. Not reviewing your client's homework indicates you speak with a 'forked-tongue': you stress the vital importance of homework and then do not bother to discuss it when your client has done it. As Beck observes: 'In our experience, if the homework is not reviewed, the patient begins to believe that it is *not* important and compliance with homework drops off dramatically' (1995: 52; original italics). Whether or not the client has completed her homework, elicit the learning from it, as we said earlier in this chapter.

If clients do not carry out their homework, monitor your own emotional reactions to non-compliance. For example, you might get angry because your client is not working as hard as you are or feel anxious because client non-compliance means you are an incompetent therapist. You will need to deal with your own disturbance-inducing thinking first before you can regain your clinical focus on tackling your clients' blocks to homework completion.

## Chapter summary

In this chapter we have considered what is involved in designing and negotiating homework tasks. Homework is the means by which clients move from intellectual insight to emotional insight into their problems, that is, they eventually internalize a rational outlook to problem-solving. The client has taken his first step in this process by agreeing to carry out his first homework assignment.

# SIX

## Working Through and Promoting Self-Change

In this final chapter, we will show how REBT therapists help their clients to generalize their learning and to internalize a self-helping philosophy whereby they take responsibility for promoting self-change.

## Working through

Working through means that, for change to occur, time and effort are required. When some clients complain that they cannot see light at the end of the tunnel (that is, the desired change) this is because they have not entered the tunnel or moved along it (that is, little, if any, action on their part has occurred). In this context, if 'therapy isn't working' it is because the client is not working to make therapy work. Moving through the tunnel is the working through phase of therapy. Grieger and Boyd state that:

> Helping clients work through their problems – that is, systematically giving up their irrational ideas – is where most of the therapist's energy and time are directed and where longlasting change takes place. Successful working through leads to significant change, whereas unsuccessful working through leads to no gain or to superficial gain at best. It is as simple as that. (1980: 122)

Your clients are unlikely to experience enduring change with their emotional problems unless they repeatedly think, feel and act against their irrational beliefs in a variety of aversive situations. In this way, multimodal disputing (D) leads to the gradual weakening of clients' irrational beliefs and the increasing strengthening of their rational beliefs to achieve new effects (E) in their thoughts, feelings and behaviours. With regard to disputing, Hauck states that:

> in all counseling one task is more critical than any other. It is self-debate. Throughout your counseling it is practically always critical that you keep the client oriented toward questioning, challenging, and debating with himself over his irrational ideas … debate, debate, debate. (1980: 244)

During the working through phase, clients, ideally, take increasing responsibility for the change process and the direction of therapy. Clients who rely on you for their progress will actually make little progress, so point out to them that you cannot do their thinking or execute their assignments for them. Grieger states that 'it is best for clients to view their RE[B]T as being a 24-hours-a-day, seven-day-a-week thing. To this end, I repeatedly tell them this' (1991: 60). On first hearing this statement, clients usually blanch at its implications, and while it is extreme, nevertheless it does point to the importance of clients working on their problems consistently rather than intermittently.

## Explaining the difference between understanding and integration

Understanding involves a client seeing how a rational outlook will lead to constructive changes in her irrational beliefs, distressing feelings and counterproductive behaviours. Understanding is associated with a weak conviction or belief in this new outlook (for example, 'I understand what you say, but I don't believe it yet'). Integration involves both understanding and action, that is, the client sees the benefits of a rational outlook and practises this outlook on a daily or frequent basis. Integration is associated with a strong conviction or belief in her rational outlook (for example, 'I understand what you're saying and I really believe it because I know it works'). From the client's viewpoint, understanding is located in the head while integration is experienced in the gut.[1] Understanding precedes integration – the former occurs in your office while the latter takes place in the client's everyday life.

To get across in a vivid way the difference between understanding and integration, ask your client how a desire to be fit is transformed into a reality or if reading a book on chess is enough to turn a person into a competent player.

## Suggest multimodal homework tasks to dispute the same irrational belief

REBT theory hypothesizes that thoughts, feelings and behaviours are interdependent and interactive processes: namely, that thoughts, feelings and behaviours will each have components of the other two modalities embedded within them. Therefore, the preferred and possibly optimal way of challenging an irrational belief and developing a rational alternative is through several modalities: cognitive, emotive, behavioural and imaginal. This multimodal approach can help to keep your clients interested in the change process and engender greater change than is likely to occur within a unimodal approach.

For example, a client, whose perfectionist standards 'are beyond reach or reason' (Burns, 1980), responds favourably to intellectual

---

[1] Understanding is equivalent to intellectual insight (rational beliefs lightly and intermittently held) and integration is equivalent to emotional insight (rational beliefs deeply and consistently held). Walen et al. suggest that

> '[e]motional insight' is a non sequitur; people do not achieve insight viscerally. When the client claims he or she has intellectual but not emotional insight, the therapist reinterprets this claim as either a problem of 'knowing' but not 'believing' the rational ideas, or of inconsistency of beliefs across time. (1992: 216)

Knowing but not believing usually occurs because clients are not acting in support of their new knowledge and, therefore, it is not integrated into their belief system. Inconsistency of beliefs across time means that in some situations a client might believe, for example, that it is not awful to make mistakes, but believes it in other situations.

disputing and reading assignments as these activities increase his awareness of the self-defeating nature of his irrational beliefs ('My perfectionist beliefs hold me back: I achieve less, not more, in my life'). However, using only one modality (cognitive, in the above example) is a narrow way of advancing personal change and is often ineffective in achieving this. In this client's case, little real change occurs as he still avoids taking on tasks he might fail at (for example, giving a presentation – behavioural) or engaging in activities where he might be seen as less than 'perfect' (for example, disclosing to others some of his imperfections – emotive). The client eventually admits that therapy is becoming 'arid' through 'all talk and no action' and that he has not in any meaningful way modified his rigid and unrealistically high standards through his present course of action (or, more accurately, inaction).

## Discuss the non-linear model of change

Some clients might assume that change, once initiated, is a smooth and uneventful process.[2] These clients have accepted the logic and wisdom of their new rational ideas in your office and now believe that they will put these ideas into immediate effect which will then lead to an immediate beneficial effect on their problems (an expected double dose of 'immediate', we might say). In order to disabuse these clients of such notions, prepare them for the vicissitudes of the change process by explaining to them the non-linear model of change. This model suggests that they will probably experience varying degrees of success in disputing their irrational beliefs in relevant contexts, they may hold themselves back from

---

[2] It is important to discuss with your clients what is involved in the change process. Do not assume it is self-evident. As Hanna points out: 'One of the fundamental mistakes made in psychotherapy and counseling is to assume that clients understand change processes. If they did, change might be accomplished much quicker and easier on a routine basis' (2002: 43).

initiating the disputing process (for example, 'I don't feel in the right mood yet'), suffer some setbacks in their efforts to change and realize that feeling better may take longer than anticipated (changes in feelings often lag behind changes in thoughts and behaviours). A realistic view of how change actually occurs can help clients to develop greater psychological resilience in tackling their problems.

Change in REBT involves clients making themselves less emotionally disturbable, but never undisturbable – we cannot transcend our fallibility no matter how much we might like to. Therefore, change is measured in relative terms, not absolute terms (for example, 'My anxiety about entering social situations has greatly diminished in terms of frequency, intensity and duration, but it has not completely gone'). Sometimes clients make themselves disillusioned about their perceived lack of progress (for example, 'I'm just the same – miserable and angry'). One way to combat this disillusionment is to encourage clients to keep a log of their thoughts, feelings and behaviours so they can pinpoint cognitive, emotive and behavioural shifts that are more gradual, even subtle, than the dramatic shifts they are hoping for. Log keeping helps them to see that improvement is taking place despite their doubts. Also, recommend to your clients Albert Ellis's (1984) pamphlet, *How to Maintain and Enhance Your Rational-Emotive Therapy Gains*, which encapsulates many of the key points of the working through process.

## Encourage your clients to transform themselves into their own therapist

From the first session onwards, you should be looking for ways to help your clients become their own therapist – the essence of REBT is self-help. If some clients baulk at the idea of self-help, remind them of this fact:

> My job is to help you help yourself. I can't do the work for you, and even if I could, you would be no better off because you would be dependent on me to sort out your present and future problems. Therapy would be like an umbilical cord that is never severed.

Transforming themselves into a self-therapist means clients using the ABCDE model to understand and tackle their problems. If your clients are successful in developing this role, you will notice a corresponding decrease in your own level of activity, for example, the client sets the agenda, uncovers and disputes her irrational thinking, designs her own homework assignments, and detects themes running through her problems such as failure or approval. With the client acting as a self-therapist, you can reconceptualize your role as a consultant, coach, trainer, mentor or adviser rather than stick to your role as a therapist. Point out to your clients that being a self-therapist is not just for present problem-solving but should, ideally, be maintained on a lifelong basis (some clients go 'off the boil' when therapy is terminated and their newly learnt self-help skills fall into disuse).

To encourage your clients to be more active in the problem-solving process, use less didactic teaching and more Socratic questioning as a means of promoting independent thinking and reducing their dependence on your problem-solving abilities. Short, probing questions can help your clients to work their way through the ABCDE model:

- 'What was the situation in which you disturbed yourself?'
- 'How did you feel at C?'
- 'What were you most upset about in that situation?'
- 'What were you telling yourself at B to feel and act in that way at C?'
- 'What effective disputes (D) did you use to challenge your irrational belief?'
- 'What would be a relevant homework assignment to tackle that belief?'
- 'What rational belief would you like to hold?'
- 'If you internalize that rational belief, what new thoughts, feelings and behaviours (E) might you experience?'

We realize that not all clients can become their own therapists in the way described above; so do not automatically expect them to take on this role. Some clients will have considerable difficulty in thinking through their problems in a more constructive way; so whatever self-help abilities they do have, endeavour to make the best use of them. For example, a client who believes that overreacting to negative comments from others is at the heart of his problem is helped to lower his level of emotional arousal by writing on a card: 'Words only hurt me if I let them'. The card acts as a continual reminder to the client that his emotional disturbance is largely self-induced.

## The use of force and energy in disputing irrational beliefs

Clients can adhere tenaciously to their irrational beliefs despite acknowledging the considerable costs that these beliefs incur (for example, high stress levels, fraught relationships). Ellis (1979b) has urged therapists to employ force and energy in helping clients to uproot their irrational beliefs and, through such modelling, clients learn to use vigour in the disputing process. Clients who challenge their irrational thinking in a tepid manner are unlikely to make a dent in such thinking, let alone dislodge it – for example, 'I suppose it wouldn't be awful if I lost my job, would it?' Such a response might not even help the client to gain intellectual insight into her fears as she is still probably convinced that it would be awful to lose her job. Force and energy helps clients to 'shake up' the cognitive status quo (that is, prise loose their rigid thinking) and develop a strong conviction in their new rational beliefs – for example, 'I don't want to lose my job but if it happens, too bad! Things will be harder for me until I find another job, but it certainly will not be the end of my world. That happens with my last breath on my deathbed.'

Having said all that, some clients will see the use of force and energy as ego-dystonic, that is, not in keeping with their self-image, and will want to challenge their irrational thinking in their own way such as 'with quiet determination', 'whittling away at it' or 'chewing things over'. Whatever approach is used, the key question is: are your client's irrational beliefs being weakened over time and with behavioural evidence to corroborate it?

## Extend situation-specific beliefs to uncover core beliefs

Clients usually subscribe to irrational beliefs in specific and general contexts. A situation-specific belief might be a person's demand that he should not have to complete his tax return as it is 'monumentally boring to do it'. A core irrational belief can be seen as a very general form of some of the situation-specific beliefs your client adheres to. With regard to the above example, the client exhibits discomfort intolerance in a variety of situations: traffic jams, waiting for lifts, meetings, gadgets not working, boring conversations, when things do not go his way, cleaning his house; the core belief underpinning these situations is, 'I absolutely shouldn't have to be inconvenienced in any way and when I am, I can't stand having to cope with it'. Tackling a core belief deals with a number of situations concurrently, whereas with a situation-specific belief, problems are resolved consecutively.

Dryden and Yankura (1995) suggest some guidelines for working with core beliefs:

### Look for common themes

While you are working on your clients' problems, particular themes often emerge that link these problems. For example, the behaviours of a client who procrastinates over a career change, stays in a relationship he is bored with, goes to the same holiday destination every year and pursues hobbies he is no longer interested in are all connected by the theme of *uncertainty*: 'I must be certain that if I make changes in my life they will turn out well for me. If they don't turn out well, my life will be awful'. Another client who engages in mind-reading with her partner, friends, colleagues, new associates is preoccupied with the theme of *approval*. 'I must know that others approve of me. If they don't, this means I'm unlikeable'. If there is a thematic continuity in your clients' problems and they have not yet pinpointed or noticed it, remember to present your ideas as hypotheses to be confirmed, modified or rejected by your clients, not as established facts.

## Encourage your clients to engage in self-observation

When your clients detect a core belief that connects a number of problems they are working on, ask them if they can point to other, as yet, undiscussed problem areas where this core belief may be operative. Such detective work can help your clients to improve considerably their cognitive awareness of the adverse impact of their core belief on many areas of their life. Some clients may be overwhelmed by the seemingly limitless number of problems confronting them; they may even terminate therapy. Therefore, this self-observation exercise should be based on your client's genuine curiosity about investigating the pervasiveness of his core belief. Do not engage in this exercise if your client is struggling to manage the problem areas that have already been identified.

## Help your clients to design a core rational philosophy

If your clients have uncovered a core irrational philosophy (for example, 'I must never show any anxiety; if I do, it means I'm weak'), then a core rational philosophy needs to be constructed to challenge it in every situation in which it is operative (for example, 'There is no reason why I must never show any anxiety. When I do show it, and I can't avoid showing it sometimes, it means I'm human, not weak'). Remember that a core rational philosophy evolves through trial and error in real-life situations and is not instantly formed in the artificial environment of your office.

## Help your clients to see how they perpetuate their core beliefs

There are three main ways in which clients perpetuate their core irrational beliefs:

### Maintenance of core irrational beliefs

This refers to ways of thinking and behaving that perpetuate core beliefs, for example, a client who sees herself as unlikeable behaves in a curt and aggressive way with others in order to protect herself from her imagined rejection by them. Unfortunately, her manner brings about the very rejection she fears and, in her mind, confirms her negative self-image.

## Avoidance of activating core irrational beliefs

This refers to the cognitive, emotive and behavioural strategies that clients use to avoid activating their core beliefs and the painful affect associated with them, for example, a client refuses to listen to rumours that his wife is having an affair or confront her about these rumours. To do so might prove that the rumours are true which, in turn, would 'prove' that he is worthless because his wife is unfaithful.

## Compensation for core irrational beliefs

This refers to the client 'fighting back' against the core belief, for example, a client who sees herself as 'not good enough' takes on many tasks to prove she is 'good enough': 'The more tasks I do will make me a better person.' However, this strategy backfires as she is overwhelmed by the work she has taken on and this puts her back at square one – 'I fight and fight but never win'.

It is important to help your clients understand their own particular ways of perpetuating their core irrational beliefs and develop robust strategies to stop the perpetuation process. In the last example above, the client realizes that trying to prove she is good enough just continually reinforces in her mind that she is not good enough. Instead of pursuing this self-defeating strategy any longer, she adopts self-acceptance as the basis of change with a strong preference to be task-competent as a measure of her performance and not 'task incontinent' to prove her worth. The client starts learning to enjoy her life rather than always trying to prove something about herself.

## Change: is it elegant?

We discussed in Chapter 1 the differences between elegant (philosophical) and inelegant (non-philosophical) change. Just to reiterate, the type of change is determined by your client, not you. By all means discuss REBT's view of what constitutes far-reaching and enduring change, but do not push for it in order to give yourself a pat on the back for doing 'proper' REBT. Change that may be disappointing for you can be highly significant for your client. After all, you have not lived your client's life or experienced the struggles he has gone through to achieve his current level of progress.

## Assessing progress

Periodically carrying out an assessment of client progress allows you to determine if your clients are on course to achieve their goals, have stalled in some way or are falling back after some initial success. In the last chapter, our client had agreed his first homework task. We now return to him to make a progress check midway through therapy.

| | |
|---|---|
| *Therapist*: | Is that 'should' of yours still rock solid? |
| *Client*: | No, it's crumbling. |
| *Therapist*: | How has that occurred? |
| *Client*: | Listening to the session recordings, talking to my wife who, like you, keeps on reminding me that what's happened has happened. I can't turn the clock back. So now I keep on reminding myself 'It happened, now move on'. |
| *Therapist*: | How can you prove to yourself that you have indeed moved on? |

[*The client has been using cognitive methods of change. The therapist wants to ascertain if this is supported by behavioural change – is the change just in his head or visible in his daily life?*]

| | |
|---|---|
| *Client*: | My anguish has gone down a lot. |
| *Therapist*: | Good, but in what specific ways has it gone down? |

[*The client has not yet provided the evidence, so the therapist continues to probe for it.*]

| | |
|---|---|
| *Client*: | I certainly brood much less and I'm more fun to be around now. I feel it within myself and certainly my wife and children tell me I'm easier to live with now. The burden is lifting. |

| Therapist: | One of the things you said would show improvement would be pottering around in the garden on these warm, summer evenings. Is that happening? |
| Client: | Definitely. We've also had a few barbecues and invited some friends round. |
| Therapist: | What about the issue of betrayal? Any new thinking there? |
| Client: | I'm convinced that he did not stab me in the back, you know, string me along knowing he was going to pull out at the last minute. |
| Therapist: | Let me ask you this: just supposing you found out that this is exactly what he did. How would you react then? |

[*The therapist is investigating whether the client's new outlook on his problem will be able to absorb this highly unpalatable fact.*]

| Client: | [*ponders*] I wouldn't like to hear it and I would be shocked if it was true but ... [*pauses*] but I would cope with it. I wouldn't go back into a state of anguish or anything like that. He has to live with what he did – that's if he did do that – and I have to make the best of things in the light of what he did. |
| Therapist: | There is a way to find out why he pulled out of the business deal. |
| Client: | I know. My wife says the same thing: contact him and find out instead of speculating about it. And that, believe it or not, is my next task. |

[*The client is setting his own homework task as part of his developing role as a self-therapist.*]

Therapist:    Good.

## Summary of the client's progress

The client said he was going to contact his former best friend to discover why he had pulled out of their proposed business deal ('Stop brooding about it and find out why'). The answer he discovered was that his best friend was experiencing severe financial difficulties at the time and could not commit himself to the deal but was too embarrassed to tell the client. The client suggested that they meet to discuss the collapse of the business deal ('I felt I was being my own therapist by taking control of the problem instead of letting the problem control me'). At the meeting, a tentative reconciliation was achieved. The client said that he was in the right frame of mind for the meeting by letting go of 'my rock-solid should', understanding the distinction between his best friend contributing to his anguish but not causing it (he had embraced emotional responsibility) and reflecting on the issue of betrayal in a less emotive way. The client said that he still wished the business deal had gone through but 'I no longer experience any anguish over it. That's good news for me and my wife.'

## Client obstacles to the working through phase

Some of the obstacles found in this phase of therapy are:

### Discomfort intolerance
We have discussed discomfort intolerance in Chapter 2, but just to recap: clients can easily disturb themselves about the often hard work to move from understanding to integration of their rational beliefs. Examples of discomfort intolerance-related beliefs are, 'I shouldn't have to work this hard to overcome my problems. I can't stand the effort involved' and 'I'm fed up with these setbacks. It's too much to put up with'. You need to encourage your clients to develop a philosophy of effort if they want to achieve their therapeutic goals (for example, 'I can stand the struggle and effort involved in change. I will persevere').

### Cognitive-emotive dissonance
This occurs when clients say they feel 'strange' or 'unnatural' as they work towards strengthening their emerging rational beliefs while simultaneously still experiencing the strong 'pull' of their old self-defeating thoughts, feelings and behaviours. This dissonant state, created by the clash or tension between the old and the new, leads some clients to terminate

therapy in order to feel 'natural again' (paradoxically, a return to their emotionally disturbed state). Cognitive-emotive dissonant reactions include clients claiming that they will lose their identity, become a phoney or turn into a machine (Grieger and Boyd, 1980).

Sloughing off the old, familiar self and acquiring a new, unfamiliar self can be uncomfortable and disorientating for some clients. Explaining to clients the basis for these dissonant reactions is enough in most cases to carry them through this stage of change (if it is not enough, then these clients will have to work harder in tolerating their cognitive-emotive dissonance until it passes: 'Focus on the benefits to come rather than on your present discomfort and strangeness').

## Pseudo-rationality (Neenan and Dryden, 1996)

Some clients, usually a small number, project a false or pretended acceptance of REBT. They are usually erudite about the theory and practice of REBT and provide the 'correct' answers to the questions you ask. However, this knowledge of REBT is not put into daily practice – it remains in the client's head; so understanding is achieved but not integration (see earlier section). Clients who display pseudo-rationality may genuinely believe that understanding alone is sufficient to effect constructive change, may like the feeling of being a 'textbook' authority on REBT or may have discomfort intolerance ideas about the hard work involved in translating REBT theory into practice. Whatever the reasons underpinning their pseudo-rationality, these clients need to internalize REBT's view of genuine rationality by committing themselves to action – and lots of it!

## 'Kangaroo' problem-solving

This means jumping from problem to problem before each one has been tackled successfully. Such an approach can lead to the fragmentation of therapy as the continuity of working through each problem is never established. To avoid this situation, agree on a coping criterion with your clients, that is, a method of assessing when they have reached the stage of managing their problems rather than mastering them. A coping criterion helps you and your clients to decide the right time to move on to the next problem.[3]

## Fear of mediocrity (Grieger and Boyd, 1980)

Clients with perfectionist traits are often reluctant to surrender their rigid 'musts' and 'shoulds' as they believe these are the source of their motivation and success in life, for example, 'If I stop driving myself in this way, my standards will plummet and my success will vanish'. In short, surrendering their 'musts' and 'shoulds' will lead to mediocrity – in their mind, the equivalent of a 'living death'. It is important to show these clients that introducing flexibility into their thinking about motivation and success does not lead to demotivation and failure. Instead, it allows them to avoid becoming overly disturbed when standards are not met or success proves temporarily elusive. From a pragmatic viewpoint, time wasted on emotional disturbance can be more usefully channelled towards problem-solving (for example, what led to an inferior performance this situation) or engaging in leisure activities (some perfectionists pursue achievement to such an extent that little time is left for anything else that might ease the pressure in their life).

## Relapse prevention

Relapse prevention helps clients to identify those future situations (for example, negative emotional states, interpersonal strife, work

---

[3] Obviously you should not be inflexible about this rule. If circumstances warrant it, you should switch to another problem before a coping criterion is reached on the previous one, for example, a crisis in the client's life; another issue on your client's problem list is deemed to be of greater clinical significance than the one initially selected. Once the switch has been made, ensure that a coping criterion is achieved on this problem before another one is discussed. If your client turns out to be a relentless 'kangaroo' problem-solver, spend time eliciting the ideas underlying her behaviour, for example, she has a low threshold for a sustained concentration on 'boring' topics.

pressures) that could trigger a return to their emotional and behavioural difficulties and teaches them coping strategies to manage these situations. Relapse prevention in REBT will be based on the skills that your clients have learnt in therapy with you. It is important to build these coping skills into your treatment plan as 'outcome is increasingly measured not only by treatment success but by relapse prevention' (Padesky and Greenberger, 1995: 70).[4]

## Criteria to decide if the working through phase of therapy has been successful

If this phase has been successful, your clients should be close to termination because they have:

1   Internalized a rational outlook and made significant reductions in the frequency, intensity and duration of their presenting problems
2   Successfully applied REBT to their presenting issues as well as other problem areas in their life
3   Identified, challenged and changed core irrational beliefs
4   Developed competence and confidence in acting as a self-therapist
5   Agreed with you that termination is near as the evidence supports this view, namely, that insight and hard work have been successfully applied to problem-solving.

However, the reality is that probably only a few clients will meet the above criteria for termination. Most clients will, for example, terminate therapy once they experience symptomatic relief rather than philosophical relief from their problems or focus only on dealing with

---

[4] Given REBT's view on our seemingly limitless ability to disturb ourselves about anything in our life, relapse reduction rather than relapse prevention would seem to us a more realistic strategy to pursue. Prevention offers more than it can probably deliver as it suggests we can always stop a full-blown reoccurrence of our original problems. Relapse reduction better describes the post-therapy progress of fallible human beings.

situation-specific irrational beliefs thereby limiting the generalizability of their therapeutic gains (of course, a problem can be strictly situation-specific as is the case with our client). You can present a rationale to your clients to stay longer in therapy in order to learn how to make themselves, generally, less emotionally disturbable but, obviously, the final decision regarding termination rests with your clients. You can offer follow-up appointments to monitor your clients' progress and see if they are maintaining their therapeutic gains. Also, clients can contact you if they encounter problems they cannot handle themselves.

## Promoting self-change

Once formal therapy has ended with your clients achieving their goals, what happens next? The answer is that therapy never ends:

> We may stop going to visit our therapist, but the process of managing our moods and behaviors is ongoing. We easily understand that we cannot make ourselves thin this year and then coast through the rest of life, eating whatever we want. We accept that we cannot get in shape with an exercise program and maintain our fitness without continued effort. In a similar way, cognitive therapy or rational-emotive living skills require maintenance. (Walen et al., 1992: 312)

Maintenance is your clients' responsibility. How do you get this message across to them? By explicitly addressing this issue: 'What do you think you need to do in order to maintain and strengthen your progress after therapy has ended?' Some clients might reply that change perpetuates itself unaided by them, 'I don't know' or that rational ideas 'sink into' their subconscious and now guide their post-therapy behaviour without any conscious effort from them. An abdication of personal responsibility for continued change or misconceptions about what is involved in this process spell trouble, that is, the decay of REBT skills through infrequent use or disuse. You might want to say something like this as a 'maintenance message' to your clients:

In therapy, you learnt two forms of responsibility: emotional and therapeutic. The former acknowledges that you are in charge of your feelings, no one else; the latter takes on the hard work of change. Both types of responsibility helped you to reach your goals. Now another form of responsibility is called for and it is even more important than the other two because it covers the rest of your life – a lifelong responsibility to protect your progress from your own forgetfulness, inaction or neglect. Without this protection, you will probably see the return of your old irrational ideas and/or the formation of new ones.

So encourage your clients to spend some time every day rehearsing their rational beliefs, looking after their mental hygiene we might say, in the same way they spend time every day attending to their physical hygiene. For example, a client with now-modified perfectionist tendencies issues a daily reminder to herself that 'good enough' is the standard to aim for in getting her work done on time and her old procrastinating-producing torment of 'never good enough' is now a distant echo. In this and other ways, self-therapy takes over from therapist-led therapy.

## Proselytizing

This means teaching REBT concepts to others not only to 'spread the word' but also for clients to deepen their own understanding of and strengthen their conviction in these concepts. Hauck urges clients not to be shy about doing this: 'Use anyone who is interested to give you opportunities to think out loud and thus improve your health. *The more you teach, the more you learn*' (1991: 100; original italics). For example, a client teaches her best friend, who asks for her advice, that losing his job is most unfortunate, not awful as he sees it, and he is not immune from experiencing such losses in his life. Such teaching helps to reinforce this point in the client's mind.

It is important in teaching REBT to others that clients do not become smug or superior (for example, 'If only you had my wisdom in these matters'); turn into a tub-thumper (that is, a ranter) or fanatic (for example, 'All other therapies are inferior'); or interrupt the conversations of

others every time they hear a 'should' or 'must' or other perceived irra-
tionalities uttered (for example, 'Why must you get that promotion?
Explain the "must" as there is no evidence for it'). Behaving like this can
turn the client into an REBT bore, turn others off the REBT viewpoint
and turn friends and colleagues in the opposite direction when they see
her coming into view (a lot of 'turning' for the client to think about!).

In order to ensure that your clients will be rational, not irrational,
proselytizers before they leave therapy, engage them in, for example,
rational role reversal to determine if they have truly grasped the REBT
view of rationality, otherwise they will be talking nonsense to others
as well as themselves (Grieger and Boyd, 1980). Explain to your clients
that it is important to select those individuals for proselytizing who
might be receptive to the REBT message, or at least willing to listen to
it, and avoid those who might be hostile to it or believe that 'all therapy is crap'. If you see your clients for follow-up or booster sessions,
discuss how successful their proselytizing efforts have been. Listen
keenly for any 'slippage' in their rational thinking which, if it has
occurred, you will need to help them correct (for example, 'You said
your friend thought it was awful, in the REBT sense, when she discovered her husband's unfaithfulness and you agreed with her. Let us
consider again the concept of awfulizing and see where you have got
yourself stuck').

## Regular psychological workouts

This means seeking out and confronting adverse situations. A robust
rational outlook may become less robust if your clients rest on their
laurels (for example, 'I've got the REBT firmly fixed in my brain. I don't
have to prove it to myself every five minutes'). We do not expect clients
to continually 'prove it' to themselves 'every five minutes' but once a
month, for example, can keep them psychologically trim. For example,
a client who believes he no longer needs the approval of others and
wishes to prove this to himself can seek out situations where he might
be criticized or ostracized for his behaviour or comments:

- Telling those of his friends who are passionately anti-Tory and make no secret of it that he votes Conservative (something he was reluctant to disclose before on 'needing approval' grounds, not because it was nobody else's business but his).
- Asking a work colleague whom previously he did not want to 'upset' to lower her voice when he is on the phone.
- Pointing out to verbose colleagues at a meeting 'that we all have busy departments to get back to, so can you make your comments concise and pertinent to the agenda' (previously he would have let the meeting drag on so as not to offend his colleagues).
- Taking a neighbour to task for playing his music too loudly (before he would have suffered in silence).

These examples are not meant to show the client becoming insensitive or cantankerous in his dealings with others (though some may see it that way), but to keep at bay his approval-seeking tendencies which slip back into his thinking from time to time ('I don't want or need to be patted on the head by others and told I'm a nice person in order to justify my existence or please others to my own detriment').

Another reason for regular psychological workouts is that some clients can slip into self-deception, that is, they believe they are maintaining their therapeutic gains when, in fact, these gains are being eroded through inaction. For example, a client who developed discomfort tolerance in order to deal with some tedious tasks in her life found, post-therapy, similar tasks piling up again through a pattern of avoidance which she justified by saying, 'I just don't want to do them, that's all. I learnt discomfort tolerance in therapy, so I have got it.'

Telling herself she had 'got it' became her rationalization for avoiding undertaking necessary but dull tasks and she eventually relapsed into discomfort intolerance ('I can't stand doing these bloody tedious things! I shouldn't have to do what I don't want to do. Why don't they go away?'). Returning to therapy for a booster session on maintaining her discomfort tolerance, convinced the client that regular psychological workouts were necessary if she wanted to keep on top of 'tedious things' in her life.

## Personal development goals

These are goals that are considered after clients have tackled their psychological problems in therapy; embarking on personal development while still psychologically disturbed means the former is likely to be undermined by the latter (for example, a client prevents herself from getting fitter by her fear that if she goes to the gym some people will poke fun at her for being overweight and becoming breathless after only a few minutes on the exercise machines). Personal development (PD) goals provide clients with new opportunities for greater personal growth and the possibility of realizing their potential (for example, becoming self-employed, writing a book, going into local politics).

Pursuing PD goals requires:

- Considerable persistence, coupled with accepting the uncertainty of whether the client's goals will be realized; for example, putting in a lot of effort may not result in her book being completed or, if completed, not being published.
- Learning from her experience and changing her behaviour if required; for example, that scribbling down a few notes occasionally when 'I'm in the mood' will not get a book written, but learning the daily discipline of writing 500 words, whether or not she is in the mood, is more likely to help her finish her book.
- Acquiring new skills if necessary; for example, learning what steps are required in selling an idea for a book to a publishing company.

Clients can schedule appointments with you (for example, every six months) to monitor their progress towards attaining their PD goals.

## Developing a rational philosophy of living

While clients may have learnt specific rational concepts (for example, non-awfulizing, self-acceptance) to tackle their particular problems, some may wish to consider developing a general rational outlook as part of their self-development. This general outlook would include:

## Thinking for oneself

This involves the client no longer accepting uncritically what others tell her and expending mental effort on deciding what is true or right for her and coming to her own conclusions, for example, 'My friend keeps on telling me I can't be happy without a man in my life. I used to let myself be persuaded by her. I'm quite happy at present without one and I'll decide what is right for me and when.'

## Learning tolerance

This means the client is willing to allow the existence of others' views but without necessarily agreeing with or liking their views. If the client finds someone else's opinion objectionable, he can argue against it without condemning the person for holding it. Tolerance also allows the client to understand that others have the right to be wrong about him without becoming upset over their comments (for example, 'We think you're the weak link in this team. What have you got to say about that?').

## Enlightened self-interest

This means the client puts his own interests first some of the time in order to remind himself that his life, not just others, needs looking after too (selfishness would be putting his interests first all of the time). If the client does not look after his own physical and psychological welfare he will not be of much use to himself or others if he becomes, for example, burnt out through excessively long hours at the office.

## Thinking and acting flexibly

Changing circumstances require adaptive responses from the client. Demanding that what exists in her life at any given moment should not exist (for example, losing a job, illness, the end of a relationship) will not make these situations easier for her to deal with. In all probability, her emotional distress will intensify if she refuses to accept the grim or frustrating reality of events (for example, depression and a withdrawal from social activity; an increase in anger). Research shows that people with good coping skills have learnt to think and act flexibly in the face of adverse events (Kleinke, 1991).

## Balancing short- and long-term interests

Living only for the present can undermine the client's longer-term interests, while forgoing all current pleasures for longer-term achievement can make his present life dull and miserable. Keeping an eye on the present as well as the future can help the client to arrive at a balance between competing interests; for example, partying and studying ensures that the client enjoys the present but also remains focused on his future prospects. Ellis sums up this balance succinctly: 'The seeking of pleasure today and the non- sabotaging of tomorrow's satisfactions' (1980c: 18).

## Learning to accept uncertainty

We live in a world of probability and chance where no absolute guarantees exist. If the client demands a certainty of outcome or success before she embarks on various activities, she is likely to become very indecisive and continually postpone action because she is overly focused on 'What if …' catastrophic thinking (for example, 'What if I take the job and don't like it? That will be awful'). Even when the client is given a guarantee, she is still doubtful because the other person could be wrong about the guarantee. Instead of continually worrying about uncertainties in life, the client can become probabilistic-minded, that is, the probability that she will get more of what she wants from life and less of what she does not want if she works hard, takes risks and is determined to forge ahead.

## Taking calculated risks

These are to be distinguished from impulsive or foolish ones. Calculated risks are based on considering the short- and long-term consequences of a particular course of action (for example, becoming self-employed) and the degree of probability of the desired outcome occurring. Risk-taking can create new and exciting possibilities for the client but also involves failures and setbacks.

A great deal of time and effort may be invested in a particular activity which turns out unfavourably; however, instead of feeling despair, the client can extract learning from the experience in order to help him make better decisions next time. Trying and sometimes failing is better than never trying at all because of a risk-averse outlook.

## Acting as a role model

Internalizing a rational outlook does not mean the client has become a paragon – far from it – but she can model what she believes is healthy behaviour for her partner and children. As Hauck observes: 'The behavior you teach and the behaviour you practice determine the kind of model you present to your loved ones' (1991: 96). The client can teach her loved ones, for example, to refrain from self-judgement (but not from judging their behaviour or performance) in order to reduce the occurrence of ego-based problems or how to stop procrastinating over making difficult decisions or carrying out unpleasant tasks.

Obviously it is important for the client to make what she says and does congruent or her loved ones will no doubt be quick to point out her hypocrisy. Acting as a role model passes on to others valuable information the client has learnt in therapy and, like anything else the client considers to be valuable, she wants others to benefit from this information.

---

## Chapter summary

In this chapter we looked at what constitutes the working through phase of therapy and described some of the obstacles to progress found there. We saw that the client had eventually internalized a rational outlook to tackle his situation-specific problem and was able to make peace with himself and, to some extent, with his former best friend. We have also discussed some of the ways clients can promote self-change after formal therapy has ended. Maintaining the momentum of change requires a lifelong commitment to hard work, but the more natural a rational outlook becomes for clients, the less effort and time will be needed from them to support it.

# A Final Word

In this book we have emphasized the importance of keeping therapy as straightforward as possible in order to concentrate clients' minds on the essence of REBT: namely, identifying, challenging and changing their disturbance-inducing thinking (such thinking, as we have said before, can be REBT-driven or idiosyncratically defined). Therapy is not served by allowing or encouraging client rambling or you engaging in long-winded and jargon-ridden explanations of REBT theory and practice, although you do need to understand the intricacies of the theory. Your guiding principle throughout therapy should be: 'To communicate REBT to my clients in a clear and concise way that will facilitate their understanding and practice of it'. Regular feedback from your clients will enable you to determine if this principle is being realized. As the philosopher John Searle observed: 'If you can't explain it clearly, then you don't understand it yourself.' Practise with fellow students, colleagues, friends and others to ensure you understand the concepts you are teaching before you teach them to your clients.

# Appendix 1
# Thinking Distortions and their Realistic Alternatives

Here we present a list of thinking distortions and their realistic alternatives showing how they stem from irrational and rational beliefs respectively. In the examples provided, the thinking distortion and realistic alternative are shown in italics.

| Thinking distortion and realistic alternative | Illustration |
|---|---|
| **Jumping to unwarranted conclusions**<br>[When something bad happens, you make a negative interpretation and treat this as a fact even though there is no definite evidence that convincingly supports your conclusions] | "Since they have seen me fail badly, as I absolutely should not have done, *they will view me as an incompetent worm*" |
| **Sticking to the facts and testing out your hunches**<br>[When something bad happens, you stick to the facts and resolve to test out any negative interpretations you may make which you view as hunches to be examined rather than as facts] | "Since they have seen me fail as I would have preferred not to do, but do not demand that I absolutely should not have done, I am not sure how they will view me. *I think that some will think badly of me, others will be compassionate towards me and yet others may not have noticed or be neutral about my failure. I can always ask them, if I want to know*" |

*(Continued)*

*(Continued)*

| Thinking distortion and realistic alternative | Illustration |
| --- | --- |
| **All-or-none thinking** [The use of black-and-white categories] | "I must not fail at any important task, *and if I do, I will only ever fail again*" |
| **Multi-category thinking** [The use of many relevant categories] | "I would like not to fail at any important task, but this does not mean that I must not do so. *If I do fail, I may well succeed and fail at important tasks in the future*" |
| **Overgeneralization** [When something bad happens, making a generalization from this experience that goes far beyond the data at hand] | "My boss must like me *and if he does not, nobody at work will like me*" |
| **Making a realistic generalization** [When something goes wrong, making a generalization from this experience that is warranted by the data at hand] | "I want my boss to like me, but he he does not have to do so. *If does not like me, it follows that other at work may or may not like me*" |
| **Focusing on the negative** [You pick out a single negative detail and dwell on it exclusively so that your vision of all reality becomes darkened, like the drop of ink that discolours the entire glass of water] | "Because I can't stand things going wrong, as they must not, *I can't see any good that is happening in my life*" |
| **Focusing on the complexity of experiences** [You focus on a negative detail, but integrate this detail into the complexity of positive, negative and neutral features of life] | "I would prefer it if things do not go wrong, but I don't have to get my desires met. When they do go wrong, I can stand it, *and I can see that my life is made up of the good, the bad and the neutral*" |

| Thinking distortion and realistic alternative | Illustration |
|---|---|
| **Disqualifying the positive** [You reject positive experiences by insisting they "don't count" for some reason or other, thus, maintaining a negative view that cannot be contradicted by your everyday experiences] | "I absolutely should not have done these foolish things and thus, *when others compliment me on the good things I have done, they are only being kind to me and forgetting these foolish things*" |
| **Incorporating the positive into a complex view of your experiences** [You accept positive experiences and locate these into the complexity of positive, negative and neutral features of life] | "I would have preferred not to have done these foolish things, but that does not mean that I absolutely should not have done them. *When others compliment me on the good things I have done, I can accept these compliments as being genuine even though I also did some foolish things which the others may also have recognized*" |

*(Continued)*

| Thinking distortion and realistic alternative | Illustration |
|---|---|
| **Mind-reading**<br>[You arbitrarily conclude that someone is reacting negatively to you, and you don't bother to check this out. You regard your thought as a fact] | "I made some errors in the Powerpoint presentation that I absolutely should not have made and *when I looked at my boss, I thought he was thinking how hopeless I was and therefore he did think this*" |
| **Owning and checking one's thoughts about the reactions of others**<br>[You may think someone is reacting negatively to you, but you check it out with the other person rather than regarding your thought as fact] | "I would have preferred not to have made some errors in the Powerpoint presentation, but that does not mean that I absolutely should not have made them. *I thought that my boss thought that I was hopeless, but I quickly realized that this was my thought rather than his and resolved to ask him about this in the morning*" |
| **Fortune-telling**<br>[You anticipate that things will turn out badly, and you feel convinced that your prediction is an already established fact] | "Because I failed at this simple task which I absolutely should not have done, *I think that I will get a very bad appraisal and thus this will happen*" |
| **Owning and checking one's thoughts about what will happen in the future**<br>[You anticipate that things may turn out badly, but you regard that as a prediction that needs examining against the available data and not as an established fact] | "I would have preferred not to have failed at this simple task, but I do not have to be immune from doing so. *I may get a very bad appraisal, but this is unlikely since I have done far more good than bad at work during the last year*" |

| Thinking distortion and realistic alternative | Illustration |
|---|---|
| **Always and never thinking**<br>[When something bad happens, you conclude that it will always happen and/or the good alternative will never occur] | "Because my present conditions of living must be good and actually are so bad and so intolerable, *they'll always be this way and I'll never have any happiness*" |
| **Balanced thinking about the future**<br>[When something bad happens you recognize that while it may happen again it is not inevitable that it will, and it is very unlikely that it will always occur. Also, you recognize that the good alternative may well occur in the future and that it is very unlikely that it will never happen] | "I would like my present conditions of living to be good, but they don't have to be that way. They are bad right now and difficult to tolerate, *but it does not follow that they will always be that way and I can be happy again*" |
| **Magnification**<br>[Here when something bad happens you exaggerate its negativity] | "I made a faux pas when introducing my new colleague which I absolutely should not have done and it's awful that I did so. *This will have a very negative effect on my career*" |
| **Keeping things in realistic perspective**<br>[Here when something bad happens, you view it in its proper perspective] | "I wish I had not made the faux pas when introducing my new colleague, but I do not have to be exempt from saying such silly things. It's bad that I did so, but hardly the end of the world *and while people may remember it for a day or two, I doubt that it will much lasting impact on my career*" |

*(Continued)*

*(Continued)*

| Thinking distortion and realistic alternative | Illustration |
| --- | --- |
| **Minimization**<br>[Here you inappropriately shrink things until they appear tiny (your own desirable qualities or other people's imperfections)] | "I must do outstandingly well and I am completely useless when I do not do so. *When I make mistakes, I am fully to blame for this and it has nothing to do with bad luck. And when I seemingly do well, this is the result of luck and anyone could have done this. However, when others make mistakes, there is a good reason for this or they were unlucky*" |
| **Using the same balanced perspective for self and others**<br>[Here when you do something good and/or others do something bad, you can recognize such behaviour for what it is] | "I want to do outstandingly well, but I do not have to do so. I am not useless when I do not so. Thus, when I make mistakes, I may be fully responsible or it may be down to bad luck. *And when I do well, this may be the result of luck, but it may be because I fully deserved to do well. When others make mistakes, they may have been unlucky or they may be fully responsible for their mistakes*" |

| Thinking distortion and realistic alternative | Illustration |
| --- | --- |
| **Emotional reasoning**<br>[You assume that your negative emotions necessarily reflect the way things really are: "I feel it, therefore it must be true"] | "Because I have performed so poorly, as I absolutely should not have done, *I feel like everybody will remember my poor performance and my strong feeling proves that they will*" |
| **Sound reasoning based on thinking and feeling** | I wish that I had not performed so poorly, but that does mean that I absolutely should not have done so. *I think and feel that people will have different responses to my performance: some negative and nasty, some compassionate and empathic and some neutral and this is probably the case*" |
| **Personalization**<br>[When a negative event occurs involving you which you may or may not be primarily responsible for, you see yourself definitely as the cause of it] | "I am involved in a group presentation and things are not going well. I am acting worse than I absolutely should act and the audience are laughing. *I am sure they are laughing only at me*" |
| **Realistic attribution**<br>[When a negative event occurs involving you which you may or may not be primarily responsible for, you acknowledge that you may be the cause of it, but you don't assume that you definitely are. Rather, you view the event from the whole perspective before making an attribution of cause that is likely to be realistic] | "I am involved in a group presentation and things are not going well. I am acting worse than I would like to do, but do not demand that I must do, and the audience are laughing. *I am not sure who or what they are laughing at and indeed, some might be laughing with us and not at us*" |

# References

Bandura, A. (1977) 'Self-efficacy: toward a unifying theory of behavioral change', *Psychological Review*, 84: 191–215.

Beck, J. S. (1995) *Cognitive Therapy: Basics and Beyond*. New York: Guilford.

Blackburn, S. (2001) *Think*. Oxford: Oxford University Press.

Burns, D.D. (1980) 'The perfectionist's script for self-defeat', *Psychology Today*, November: 34–57.

Burns, D. D. (1989) *The Feeling Good Handbook*. New York: William Morrow.

Cormier, W. H. and Cormier, L. S. (1985) *Interviewing Strategies for Helpers*, second edition. Monterey, CA: Brooks/Cole.

DiGiuseppe, R. (1989) (audio cassette recording) *What Do I Do With My Anger: Hold It In or Let It Out?* New York: Albert Ellis Institute for Rational Emotive Behavior Therapy.

DiGiuseppe, R. (1991) 'Comprehensive cognitive disputing in RET', in M. E. Bernard (ed.), *Using Rational-Emotive Therapy Effectively: A Practitioner's Guide*. New York: Plenum. pp. 173–95.

Dryden, W. (1985) 'Challenging but not overwhelming: a compromise in negotiating homework assignments', *British Journal of Cognitive Psychotherapy*, 3 (1): 77–80.

Dryden, W. (1986) 'A case of theoretically consistent eclecticism: humanizing a computer "addict"', *International Journal of Eclectic Psychotherapy*, 5 (4): 309–27.

Dryden, W. (1991) *A Dialogue with Albert Ellis: Against Dogma*. Milton Keynes: Open University Press.

Dryden, W. (1994) *10 Steps to Positive Living*. London: Sheldon Press.

Dryden, W. (1997) *Therapists' Dilemmas*, revised edition. London: SAGE.

Dryden, W. (1998a) 'Understanding persons in the context of their problems: a rational emotive behaviour therapy perspective', in M. Bruch and

F. W. Bond (eds), *Beyond Diagnosis: Case Formulation Approaches in CBT*. Chichester: Wiley. pp. 43–64.

Dryden, W. (1998b) *Are You Sitting Uncomfortably?* Ross-on-Wye: PCCS Books.

Dryden, W. (2001) *Reason to Change: A Rational Emotive Behaviour Therapy (REBT) Workbook*. Hove: Brunner–Routledge.

Dryden, W. (2009) *Rational Emotive Behaviour Therapy: Distinctive Features*. London: Routledge.

Dryden, W. and Yankura, J. (1995) *Developing Rational Emotive Behavioural Counselling*. London: SAGE.

Ellis, A. (1969) 'A weekend of rational encounter', in A. Burton (ed.), *Encounter: The Theory and Practice of Encounter Groups*. San Francisco, CA: Jossey–Bass. pp. 112–27.

Ellis, A. (1976) 'The biological basis of human irrationality', *Journal of Individual Psychology*, 32: 145–68.

Ellis, A. (1979a) 'Discomfort anxiety: a new cognitive behavioural construct: Part I', *Rational Living*, 14 (2): 3–8.

Ellis, A. (1979b) 'The issue of force and energy in behavior change', *Journal of Contemporary Psychotherapy*, 10: 83–97.

Ellis, A. (1980a) 'Discomfort anxiety: a new cognitive behavioral construct: Part 2', *Rational Living*, 15 (1): 25–30.

Ellis, A. (1980b) 'The value of efficiency in psychotherapy', *Psychotherapy: Theory, Research and Practice*, 17: 414–18.

Ellis, A. (1980c) 'An overview of the clinical theory of rational-emotive therapy', in R. Grieger and J. Boyd (eds), *Rational-Emotive Therapy: A Skills-Based Approach*. New York. Van Nostrand Reinhold. pp. 1–31.

Ellis, A. (1984) *How to Maintain and Enhance Your Rational-Emotive Therapy Gains*. New York: Albert Ellis Institute for Rational Emotive Behavior Therapy.

Ellis, A. (1986) (audio cassette recording) *Unconditionally Accepting Yourself and Others*. New York: Albert Ellis Institute for Rational Emotive Behavior Therapy.

Ellis, A. (1994) *Reason and Emotion in Psychotherapy*, second edition. New York: Birch Lane Press.

Ellis, A. (1999) *How to Make Yourself Happy and Remarkably Less Disturbable*. Atascadero, CA: Impact Publishers.

Gilbert, P. (2000) *Counselling for Depression,* second edition. London: SAGE.

Grieger, R. (1991) 'Keys to effective RET', in M. E. Bernard (ed.), *Using Rational-Emotive Therapy Effectively: A Practitioner's Guide.* New York: Plenum. pp. 35–67.

Grieger, R. and Boyd, J. (1980) *Rational-Emotive Therapy: A Skills-Based Approach.* New York: Van Nostrand Reinhold.

Hanna, F. J. (2002) *Therapy with Difficult Clients.* Washington, DC: American Psychological Association.

Hauck, P. (1980) *Brief Counseling with RET.* Philadelphia, PA: Westminster Press.

Hauck, P. (1991) *Hold Your Head Up High.* London: Sheldon Press.

Hjelle, L. A., and Ziegler, D. J. (1992) *Personality Theories: Basic Assumptions, Research and Applications.* New York: McGraw–Hill

Kleinke, C. L. (1991) *Coping with Life Challenges.* Pacific Grove, CA: Brooks/Cole.

Lazarus, A. A. (1981) *The Practice of Multimodal Therapy.* New York: McGraw–Hill.

Maultsby, Jr, M. C. and Ellis, A. (1974) *Technique for Using Rational-Emotive Imagery.* New York: Albert Ellis Institute for Rational Emotive Behavior Therapy.

Meichenbaum, D. (1985) *Stress Inoculation Training.* New York: Pergamon Press.

Neenan, M. and Dryden, W. (1996) *Dealing with Difficulties in Rational Emotive Behaviour Therapy.* London: Whurr.

Neenan, M. and Dryden, W. (2000) *Essential Rational Emotive Behaviour Therapy.* London: Whurr.

Neenan, M. and Dryden, W. (2001) *Learning From Errors in Rational Emotive Behaviour Therapy.* London: Whurr.

Neenan, M. and Dryden, W. (2002) *Cognitive Behaviour Therapy: An A–Z of Persuasive Arguments.* London: Whurr.

Padesky, C. A. and Greenberger, D. (1995) *Clinician's Guide to Mind Over Mood.* New York: Guilford.

Passons, W. R. (1975) *Gestalt Approaches in Counseling.* New York: Holt Rinehart and Winston.

Persons, J. B. (1989) *Cognitive Therapy in Practice: A Case Formulation Approach.* New York: Norton.

Rogers, C. R. (1957) 'The necessary and sufficient conditions of therapeutic personality change', *Journal of Consulting Psychology*, 21: 95–103.

Walen, S. R., DiGiuseppe, R. and Dryden, W. (1992) *A Practitioner's Guide to Rational-Emotive Therapy*, second edition. New York: Oxford University Press.

Wessler, R. A. and Wessler, R. L. (1980) *The Principles and Practice of Rational-Emotive Therapy.* San Francisco, CA: Jossey–Bass.

Woods, P. J. (1991) 'Orthodox RET taught effectively with graphics, feedback on irrational beliefs, a structured homework series, and models of disputation', in M. E. Bernard (ed.), *Using Rational-Emotive Effectively: A Practitioner's Guide.* New York: Plenum. pp. 69–109.

# Index

ABC model 4, 18–19
  A/critical A 19, 20–3
  B/beliefs 19, 23
    irrational 29–34
    rational 24–9
  C/consequences 19
    behavioural 35
    emotional 34–5
    thinking 36
  putting into practice 40–2
  the situation 19, 20
  teaching/explaining to client 37–8
acceptance belief 27–9
arguments, types of 13
assessment
  clients' stories
    listening to 39–40
    putting into ABC framework 40–2
  explaining REBT 37–9
  focus on emotional responsibility
    43–4
  goal setting 44–5
  meta-emotional problems 45–6
awfulizing belief 31–2

behavioural change 15
behavioural tasks 64–5
beliefs
  and choice-based constructivism 8
  extreme vs non-extreme 5
  irrational 29–34
  beliefs levels of abstraction 48–9
  rational 24–9

case formulation 10–11
change 14–16, 77, 83–4
  client control of 52
  compromises in therapeutic
    change 15–16
  integration vs understanding
    75–6, 97
  maintaining see relapse
    prevention
  major dimensions of 44
  non-linear model of 77–8
  working through and 74–5
cognitive distortion 36
cognitive tasks 61–4
cognitive–emotive dissonance
  86–7
conclusions, jumping to 99
consequences see ABC model
constructive behaviour 35
core irrational beliefs 18, 49, 81
  identifying/dealing with 81–3
  perpetuating 82–3
  and self-observation 82
critical A see ABC model

depreciation see self-esteem
development, personal 11–12
didactic style 13
discomfort 7
  intolerance belief 32–3, 86
  tolerance belief 26–7
disputing 47–8, 54–9
  approaches to 59
    creative disputing 50–3

disputing *cont.*
    formulaic disputing 49–50
    improvisation 53
    belief levels 48–9
    preparing clients for 53–4
    role of force and energy in
        14–15, 80
    types of arguments 13
dissatisfaction 11–12
disturbed feelings 7, 11–12
    recording 44–5
dogmatism 24–5

eclecticism 17
efficiency, therapeutic 16–17
ego domain 7
Ellis, A. 1, 78
embarrassment-attacking exercises
    65–6
emotions
    disturbed feelings
        7, 11–12, 44–5
    emotional reasoning 105
    emotional responsibility 43–4
    emotive tasks 65–6
    healthy and unhealthy 5–6, 34–5
empirical arguments 13
enactive style 14

feelings *see* emotions
flexible beliefs 4–5, 9, 96
fortune-telling 102

gains, maintaining
    self-help pamphlet 78
    *see also* relapse prevention
generalization 100
goals
    establishing 44–5
    links with homework 68
    personal development 94
gradualism 14

happiness assignments 67
healthy negative emotions 5–6, 34–5
homework 60–1
    assignment tasks
        behavioural 64–5
        cognitive 61–4
        emotive 65–6
        imagery 66
    multimodal approaches 76–7
    negotiating and enabling 67–72
    non-compliance 61, 70–1, 71,
        71–2, 72–3
human nature 2–3, 8
human worth 6
humour 10, 14

imagery tasks 66
inferences, distorted 6
inferential change 15
informality 10
informed consent 37
integration 75–6, 87
irrational beliefs 36
    biological basis for 8
    changing to rational 12, 47–8
    early focus on 12
    thinking distortions
        listed 99–105
    *see also* disputing

'kangaroo' problem solving 87–8

listening homework 62–3
logical arguments 13
long-term interests 96

mediocrity, fear of 88
mental health 8–9
meta-emotional problems 7, 44,
    45–6
metaphorical style 14
mind-reading 102

multimodal disputing 76–7
'musts and shoulds' 42, 88

non-awfulizing belief 25–6
non-critical A 22–3
non-linear change 77–8

perfectionism 88
personalization 105
postmodern relativism 2
pragmatic arguments 13
preference, non-dogmatic 24–5
progress, assessing 84–5
proselytizing 91–2
pseudo-rationality 87
psycho-educational focus 11, 15
psychological workouts 92–3

questioning styles 13–14

rationality 82
    biological basis of 8
    and philosophy of living 15, 94–7
reading homework 62
REBT, overview of 1
    practical features 9–17
    simple explanation of 37–9
    theoretical features 2–9, 17
relapse prevention 88–9
    personal development goals 94
    promoting self-change 90–1
    proselytizing 91–2
    psychological workouts 92–3
    rational philosophy of living 94–7
rigid beliefs 5, 8, 29–31
risk-taking 96–7
    activities 64
role model 97

secondary disturbance 7
self-change, promoting 75, 90–1

self-efficacy 69
self-esteem/depreciation 7, 33–4
    emotive exercises 65–6
self-interest, enlightened 95
self-therapy 77–8, 78–80
shame-attacking exercises 65–6
short-term interests 96
situation-specific beliefs 48–9, 59
    and uncovering core
        beliefs 81–3
situational change 16
Socratic questioning 13
'stay-in-there' exercises 64
storytelling 38–40

teaching and learning 11, 15
    client proselytizing 91–2
    client self-help 77–8, 78–80
    explaining REBT 37–9
termination 89
therapeutic efficiency 16–17
therapeutic relationship 9–10
therapeutic styles 13–14
thoughts/thinking
    constructive vs unconstructive 36
    thinking distortions 36, 99–105
    thinking for oneself 95
tolerance 95
trying vs doing 69–70

uncertainty 96
unconditional acceptance 6, 10
unconstructive behaviour 35
unhealthy negative emotions 5–6,
    34–5

working through phase 74–5
    client obstacles to 86–8
    criteria of success 89–90
writing homework 63–4
    log keeping 78